R. H. Stelle

with Compliments of

L. W. Brodhead

June 1873

THE

DELAWARE WATER GAP:

ITS SCENERY,

ITS LEGENDS AND EARLY HISTORY.

BY

L. W. BRODHEAD.

Scenes must be beautiful which, daily viewed,
Please daily, and whose novelty survives
Long knowledge and the scrutiny of years.

COWPER.

PHILADELPHIA:
SHERMAN & CO., PRINTERS.
1870.

PHILADELPHIA:
CAXTON PRESS OF SHERMAN & CO.

PREFACE

TO THE FIRST EDITION.

The frequent demand for a book descriptive of the scenery and the places of interest about the Water Gap, has induced the preparation of this little volume.

The addition of some historical account of the place, historical notes, &c., to the object first contemplated, it is thought, will afford interest to a portion, at least, of its readers.

The story of Lover's Leap is given to supply the numerous calls from the younger and more romantic portion of the visitors at the Water Gap for a recital of the legend connected with that place, and which could not always be satisfactorily rendered. It does not aspire to the dignity of an independent romance, and the introduction of more than the leading actors in the story was purposely avoided, that too much space might not be occupied in illustrating certain historical incidents, for which there is little authentic data; but which are believed, however, to contain some elements of truth.

The beautiful Legend, written by Mrs. E. S. Swift, will be read with interest and pleasure. In granting permission for its publication in this connection, that lady says: "I love every foot of ground at the Water Gap; to me it is full of pleasing memories. I suppose I shall find the place very much altered,—improved, people tell me; but Nature has been so lavish in her loveliness there, I do not think it could bear improvement. I shall be glad to see your book published: it has long been wanted; the Water Gap being, of late, as familiar as household words."

The hurried preparation of these pages has led to the contemplation of a larger volume, which may ere long appear, giving a more complete topographical and historical account of the Water Gap, together with a History of the Upper Valley of the Delaware.

It will be difficult for those who read what is here given, to divest their minds of the opinion that it is written in the interest of the Kittatinny House. The relation the writer sustains to the place would make the inference natural, hence much delicacy is felt in placing it before the public; but he hopes for a more liberal appreciation of his motives on the part of the intelligent class of readers who visit the Water Gap.

He has only attempted to furnish that which those who visit the place constantly demand, and which he has failed in inducing those more experienced and more competent than himself to undertake.

Less mention, however, is made of the House itself than one less interested would, perhaps, have given; and as to the places described, they have but to be visited to justify all that is said in their praise.

To the author this maiden effort has been but a labor of love,—the anticipation of gain in any form having no impulse,—as most of the places described were the play-grounds of his boyhood, the rambles of his youth, and are the admiration of his manhood.

Delaware Water Gap, 1867.

SECOND EDITION.

THE second edition is now presented, revised and enlarged.

The historical matter relating to the Upper Valley of the Delaware, proposed to be included in this edition, was found, on partial preparation, to greatly exceed the limits contemplated, and will, therefore, be published in a separate volume.

The narrative, "Lost on the Mountain," was written by request of friends of the lady in Philadelphia, and contains all the facts relating to that exciting local incident.

The sketch of the Minisink and its early people, family genealogy, Indian antiquities, &c., here given will be understood as merely introductory, with the hope that these subjects will awaken an interest in those who can assist the author with data for their successful completion.

DELAWARE WATER GAP, 1870.

CONTENTS.

SCENERY.

	PAGE
GUIDE,	xi
Delaware River,	12
Delaware Water Gap,	16
Kittatinny House,	22
Rebecca's Bath,	23
Eureka Falls,	23
Moss Grotto,	23
Caldeno Creek,	28
Cooper's Cliff,	30
Table Rock,	31
Moss Cataract,	33
Diana's Bath,	33
Caldeno Falls,	33
Lover's Leap,	36
The Hunter's Spring,	38
Prospect Rock,	39
Summit of Mount Minsi,	40

PAGE

Sapper's and Miners, ... 41
The Gaps in the Mountain, ... 44
The Indian Interpreter (Tatamy), ... 44
The Rev. David Brainerd, ... 45
Mount Tammany, or New Jersey Summit, ... 48
Indian Chief, Tamanend, ... 48
Sunset Hill, ... 50
Mount Caroline, ... 53
Laurel Hill, ... 54
Blockhead Mountain, ... 55
Lovers' Retreat, or the Haunted Pine, ... 56
Martin's Rest, ... 59
Church of the Mountain, ... 59

CARRIAGE DRIVES.

Cherry Valley and Fox Hill, ... 74
Stroudsburg, ... 75
Cherry Valley and Crystal Hill, ... 76
Buttermilk Falls, ... 77
Marshall's Falls, ... 78
Bushkill Falls, ... 79
Falls of Winona, ... 83
Transue's Knob, ... 84
Castle Rock, ... 85
New Jersey Hills, ... 86
Lake of the Mountain, ... 86
Indian Relics, ... 87
Indian Graves, ... 115

LEGENDS.

PAGE

Winona; or, the Story of Lover's Leap, ... 125
Legend of the Delaware Water Gap, by Mrs. E. S. Swift, ... 158
Passage of the Delaware through the Blue Ridge, by Dr. William B. Dey, ... 190
Lost on the Mountain, ... 193

HISTORICAL.

Sketch of the Minisink and its early People, . . . 214
Early Settlements in the Minisink, ... 233
Depui Family, ... 236
Van Campen Family, ... 239
Brodhead Family, ... 241
Stroud Family, ... 250
Early Settlements at the Delaware Water Gap, . . . 254
First Visitors, ... 262
Durham Boats, ... 264
Steamboat "Alfred Thomas," 266
First Telegram, ... 269
Railroads, ... 270
Extract from a Letter of M. R. Hulce, Esq., . . . 273
Extract from a Letter of C. L. Pascal, Esq., . . . 274

GUIDE

TO THE PLACES OF INTEREST.

Delaware Water Gap.

See from the river in boats, from the carriage-road, from Table Rock and Lover's Leap.

Rebecca's Bath—Eureka Falls—Moss Cataract.

Follow down the carriage-road in the direction of the Gap to the first creek.

Cooper's Cliff—Table Rock—Diana's Bath—Moss Cataract—Caldeno Falls.

Pass through the gate in front of the Hotel, ascend the first rise of ground, turn to the right, and take the direction of the *White lines*, which can be seen on every suitable rock and tree.

Lover's Leap.

Follow the direction of the Red lines till you intersect the *Blue* in the path leading to the *Left*.

The Hunter's Spring.

Follow the Red lines till you intersect the *White* leading to the *Right*.

Prospect Rock.

Follow the Red lines till you intersect the *Yellow* leading to the Left.

Mount Minsi, or the Pennsylvania Summit.

Follow the Red lines.

Sunset Hill.

Follow the direction of the *Yellow lines* at the eastern end of the inclosure in front of the Hotel.

Mount Caroline.

Follow up the carriage-road in the direction of the village, and ascend the highest peak in the rear of the church.

Laurel Hill,

Is in front of Mount Caroline, and east of the School-house.

Mount Tammany, or New Jersey Summit.

Ascend from the opposite bank of the river, below the Slate Factory.

Lake of the Mountain.

Take carriage to Shawnee; ascend the mountain from the opposite bank of the river under direction of a guide.

☞ Persons taking any of the carriage-rides without a driver, will obtain directions from the person having the carriages in charge.

☞ For a more full direction, see description of the places you wish to visit.

THE

Delaware Water Gap.

SCENERY.

Delaware River.

LITTLE rivulets dripping from rock to rock down the western slope of the Catskill Mountain form at its base two wild streamlets, too small and uncertain at first to assume "a local habitation and a name," but being fed by numberless little accessories, at length emerge the *Mohawk* and *Popacton*,—the west and east branches of the Delaware. Rejoicing in their new creation, and gaily dancing in the sunlight down declivities, forming here and there tumultuous cascades, or gurgling through ravines, wander away from their beautiful mountain source.

In parallel windings they flourish and grow self-sustaining and self-important, like youth at their first departure from the parental mansion. Away they glide through forest and hidden wilds, such as where the hart goeth "panting after the water brooks," and on, on, until the music of their cascades reverberated from the steep mountain-side is lost in the distance. A hundred miles away, like plighted lovers, they meet, embrace, and are commingled in one.

From such a beautiful source and from such small beginnings, we have the noble old Delaware, the poetry of rivers, and the love and admiration of its "original people."

The point of junction is near the northeast corner of Pennsylvania, and the united streams thereafter form its eastern boundary. The place of the union of these streams, in the language of the Indians, was beautifully significant. It was called by them *Shehawkan,* meaning "the wedding of the waters." At this point, after having wandered so far from its parent mountain, and, as if desirous of returning again for protection, the stream diverges in a southeasterly direction, and rapidly moving onward receives the waters of the Lackawaxen (*Lechauwek'sink*), whose wild ravines echo the songs of the merry raftmen. Approaching the Blue Ridge at right angles it reaches it again at the junction of the three States,* having journeyed in its wild rambles one hundred and fifty miles, yet being only half that distance from its source. Along the western base of the mountain it flows majestically onward, lighting up field and forest, and adding a charm to a hundred landscapes, diverging from the "blue hills" at times to give our New Jersey neighbors a portion of the rich valley, and again washing their rocky base, and receiving the waters of the Bushkill fresh from its little Niagara, and then Brodhead's and Marshall's Creeks (the prolific sources of the speckled trout), the unwearied stream at length reaches the Water Gap to add the climax to its beautiful creations.

The forty miles of the course of this stream

* Near Port Jervis. It was at this point a gentleman once asserted on a wager that he could prove to the satisfaction of all present, that he had been in *five States* on that day. It was easy to see how he could have been in Pennsylvania, New York, and New Jersey, but the other two were not so clear, till he explained that in the morning he had been in a state of *single unblessedness*, and was now in a state of *double felicity*.

along the base of the mountain from Port Jervis to this place, is unsurpassed in the variety and beauty of the pictures it presents; and taken in connection with the fine character of the roads, the numerous waterfalls adjacent, there is not perhaps a more desirable drive of the same extent along any river in the country.

Delaware Water Gap.

The great geological phenomenon bearing the above expressive though not very euphonious name, is one of the most striking scenes in our country, and is a subject upon which volumes might be written. The chain of mountains known in general terms as the *Blue Ridge,* ranging nearly parallel with the Atlantic coast, and having its rise in New Hampshire and terminating in the extreme Southern States, has, in each State through which it passes, some distinguishing feature, as the *White Mountains* in New Hampshire, *Green Mountains* in Vermont, *Catskill* in New York, *Harper's Ferry* in Virginia, and the *Delaware Water Gap* in Pennsylvania and New Jersey.

The waters of the Delaware at this point approach the mountain with a gentle current, and gracefully sweeping from the north toward the east, turn suddenly and pass through the Blue Ridge, cutting it to the base, while its ragged, sloping sides towering up to an elevation of 1600 feet, frown down upon the river as it calmly pursues its course toward the ocean.

Whether this immense chasm has been caused by one mighty eruption, or by a gradual yielding of stratum after stratum, by the immense pressure of the waters of a lake thousands of acres in area, down to the present bed of the river; or by the active dissolution of the material upon which the foundation of the mountain rested, burying the whole mass deep in the gulf thus created, is of course a subject of mere conjecture, and can never be satisfactorily determined. The depth and solidity of the stratification on either side of the chasm would seem, however, to favor the first hypothesis.

The evidences of the action of water on rocks hundreds of feet above the present level of the river-bed, and the masses of drift forming isolated hills and alluvial banks, indicate lake-like repose in the country now drained by the tributaries of the stream above the great gate in the mountain barrier.

The Indian name of *Minisink*,—meaning "the water is gone,"—given by the aborigines to the level country north of the Gap, and extending up the river many miles, would seem to indicate some tradition confirming the theory of a lake at some remote period of time.

The mass of matter thrown out from this chasm must have deluged the whole country south of the "Gap" for many miles in extent; but we shall, perhaps, never find a *Herculaneum* or a *Pompeii* buried beneath the accumulated *debris,* although some future *Boucher de Perthes,* delving deep in the bowels of the earth for evidences of *pre-historic* man, may here find some relic of the *stone age,* very like those now so plentifully found upon the surface.

The two following paragraphs, giving an estimate of the probable amount of matter thrown out of the opening forming the "Gap," &c., are extracts from a letter written by the author of this book, some years ago, for the *New York Sun*, portions of which were afterward published in a History of Northampton and Monroe Counties:

"Estimating the height of the mountain on either side at 1600 feet, the width of the space or distance between the mountains at half their height to be 1000 feet, the whole distance through at one mile, would give the enormous amount of 8,451,600,000 cubic feet, a sufficiency of matter to overwhelm a township of ordinary size to the depth of five feet.

"Here there has been a convulsion that must have *shaken the earth to the very centre,* and the 'elements to give signs that all was lost.' But He who governs the world and has all things at His command; He who holds the globe by the might of His power, can remove the mountains from their foundations and bury them in the deep, and the great machinery of the universe continue to move and lose none of its functions."

The wonderful phenomena of nature witnessed in every clime, setting at defiance all human theories and human research, seem to exist only to impress us with the majesty of Omnipotence, and our own fallible insufficiency; and the great geological transformations that have taken place in the primary condition of the earth's surface, and the constant mutations still continuing, together with our own wasting lives, admonish us of the instability of all sublunary things, and that ere long,

> "Like the baseless fabric of this vision,
> The cloud-capp'd towers, the gorgeous palaces,
> The solemn temples, the great globe itself,
> Yea, all which it inherit, shall dissolve,
> And, like this unsubstantial pageant faded,
> Leave not a rack behind."

The Delaware Water Gap may have been so planned from creation. We are told in the beautiful language of inspiration: that, "He putteth forth his hand upon the rocks, He overturneth the mountains by the roots, He cutteth out rivers among the rocks, and His eye seeth every precious thing."

The Gap should be seen from the *river*, from *Table Rock, Lover's Leap*, and from the *carriage-road*. Taking a small boat, at the foot of the cliff on which the hotel is situated, and rowing down over the quiet waters, affords, perhaps, the most impressive view, such as you will ever remember with pleasure. You can better realize the height of the mountain, the width of the chasm, the serpentine course of the river, and the force required to produce the dislocation.

The Gap is also seen to good advantage by walking down the carriage-road. By continuing the walk to the Point of Rocks, you have the view from a variety of aspects, each of which is a study, and must give interest and pleasure to the commonest perceptions. To the geologist and the botanist, this is a fine field for the exercise of either talent. On the return, you have a view up the Delaware, which, though of an entirely different character, is a pleasing and interesting one.

Few persons from the cities see the Water Gap in winter, and, therefore, lose some of the grandest scenes the place affords. The snows of the entire season accumulate to the depth of several feet on the top and sides of the mountain, appearing like an immense white curtain studded with clumps of evergreen trees, suspended from the summit of the Pennsylvania Mountain, and reaching to its base, of the dimensions of 1600 feet in height by one mile in length, as seen from the hotel. The ice in the Gap acquires great solidity and thickness, and presents an impenetrable barrier to that which is brought down from the upper waters, by the first winter freshets. It accumulates here in immense bodies, and is piled up in confused masses, as high as the grading of the railroad, unable to force the solid masonry of winter in the narrow gorge between the mountains. It is not uncommon to see these broken cakes of ice piled up to the height of twenty feet above the water, some pieces standing upright from ten to fifteen feet above the general mass. This condition continues until the return of warmer weather, when the gateway is forced, and the whole body passes out with a crashing sound, distinctly heard at the hotel.

Kittatinny House.

On the side of the Pennsylvania Mountain is a series of plateaux or geological steps, and on the first of these, at an elevation of 180 feet above the river, stands the Kittatinny House. The spot commands a fine view of the windings of the river, and the surrounding mountains and hills; but the view of the Gap itself is incomplete, being obstructed, at this point, by "Blockhead" Mountain, which, however, is overlooked by the views from other points higher up the side of the mountain. The situation is well chosen, and has the benefit of every breeze. The hotel buildings are large, though not sufficiently so to accommodate the annually increasing number of visitors, and more extensive accommodations are in contemplation. The places of interest, hereinafter to be described, are mostly in the immediate vicinity of the hotel. There are several boarding-houses, distant from half a mile to three miles from the Kittatinny House, viz.: "Brainerd House," by Thomas Brodhead; "Lenape House," by A. B. Burrell; "Glenwood House," by Samuel Alsop; "River Farm House," by Evan T. Croasdale; "Analoming House," by James Bell; and "Highland Dale House," by Charles Foulk; also several houses at Stroudsburg, a pleasant town four miles distant.

Rebecca's Bath—Eureka Falls—Moss Grotto.

On the road, about halfway between the hotel and the Point of Rocks, is the Echo.

The return of the voice from the opposite mountain in New Jersey is well defined at the parapet which borders the road. Here you cross a little stream, now perhaps very modest, gentle, and almost noiseless; yet so sparkling and bewitching, half hidden under the canopy of greenwood, and at times disappearing between the moss-covered rocks, that you almost fear, in its wild rambles, such "a thing of beauty" cannot be "a joy forever." But it murmurs on, in summer's heat and winter's cold; more voluminous at times, but never less beautiful. So coy, so fickle, and yet so lovely and fascinating, how very apt are we to compare it to one, in our mind, of the lovelier part of our creation. And it has, too, its seasons of frolic and gayety. Now, whilst I write, "winter's icy chains have bound it," and the deep snows have borne down the branches of the trees that skirt its way, till they dip low in the stream, and are festooned with icy pearls that glitter in the sunlight, and almost make you sad to think they cannot endure; but a few warm sunny days "unbinds the silver rill," and behold the modest little rivulet with the proportions and the roar of a cataract!

Up this ravine are located "Rebecca's Bath," "Eureka Falls," and "Moss Grotto." The stream has its rise high up the side of the mountain, at "The Hunter's Spring," and the rays of the sun are shut out for the whole distance, causing the growth of mosses and ferns to be uncommonly beautiful, and the strong current of air following down the course of the stream, makes the summer days at *Eureka* like those of autumn elsewhere.

The railroad, though a great improvement over the old method of reaching the Water Gap by stage-coach, has nevertheless made some innovations upon the primitive beauty of the place, that are not pleasant to contemplate; besides destroying that charming walk once studded with sycamores, free from underbrush and turfed with green, situated between the base of the cliff on which the hotel rests and the river, which the earlier visitors delighted in calling "Love Lane," it has forced the carriage-road so far up the ravine, at Rebecca's Bath, as to destroy much of its former beauty, and caused the demolition of many grand old trees below it, and all along the river-bank, under whose shelter passed the carriage-road of former days.

The following account of the exploration of these places was written by the late lamented W. Arthur Jackson in the Hotel Register, in 1852. "*The Bridge of Sighs,*" alluded to in this record, heaved its last expiring breath at the first sight of the Irishman with his pickaxe and shovel. The place was destroyed in the construction of the present carriage-road:

"NOTICE TO VISITORS.

"*Monroe County, ss.*

"Be it remembered that on the twenty-seventh day of August, A.D. 1852, the following named persons, to wit: Miss R. D. Smith, Miss Elizabeth Nixon, Miss Lizzie Nixon, Mr. F. C. Foster, Mr. Wm. S. Baker, and Mr. W. A. Jackson, all of the City of Philadelphia, or now, or late there residing, did with great *toil, labor, work,* and *diligence, discover, lay out, survey,* and *explore,* a certain waterfall, cascade, cataract, stream, basin, and grotto, being and lying within the bounds of the county aforesaid, and with divers in struments and tools, to wit: one dull axe, one sharp hatchet, two jack-knives, and one pine tree, did thereto, and thereabout, build, construct, and open a certain path or public highway, for the use and benefit of all foot passengers and pedestrians forever; and did, upon and over the said stream, erect a certain bridge or causeway of rocks; and then and there, by virtue of the powers, privileges, and immunities in them as discoverers of the said location, by the laws of nations vested, did thereto assign the following names, to wit: to the said falls, the name of *Eureka Falls;* to the said bridge of rocks, the name of *The Bridge of Sighs;* to the said bath or basin, the name of *Rebecca's Bath;* and to the said grotto, the name of *Moss Grotto.*

"And moreover, at the same time and place above mentioned, it was, by the said parties then and there assembled, unanimously resolved and determined that the said Falls, Bath, Grotto, and Bridge, so as aforesaid more particularly named and described, were, and the same are pronounced and decreed, and shall ever hereafter be deemed and taken to be, in all respects, superior to all other Falls, Baths, Bridges, and Grottos whatsoever and wheresoever situated within ten miles circular of the home and habitation of William A. Brodhead, Proprietor of the House commonly known as the Kittatinny House.

"Witness the hands and seals of the said parties hereunto subscribed, the day and year last aforesaid.

MISS R. D. SMITH, [L. S.]
MISS NIXON, [L. S.]
MISS LIZZIE NIXON, [L. S.]
FRANK C. FOSTER, [L. S.]
W. ARTHUR JACKSON, [L. S.]
WM. S. BAKER, [L. S.]"

Under this, some justly complaining individual has written the following:

"The Falls may have their name from you,
And be worthy of survey;
But yet, we think, 'tis justly due
To point us out the way."

Caldeno Creek.

Caldeno Creek has its rise high up the side of Mount Minsi. After tumbling down its rocky precipices, it at length finds its way into the valley, and after gladdening the inmates of two or three scattered farmhouses, runs close up to the ruins of an old saw-mill, still offering to render willing service as of yore, when it turned its limpid summersaults around the giddy wheel, and reminding its old companion of the lively times they once enjoyed together; but the old mill being too dilapidated to respond, the stream heaves a sigh over departed greatness, and passes on, meandering through a meadow, dallying in little eddies to give the trout a chance to bask in the sunshine, and again hides itself in the thick woods. Cooled and purified it emerges again at Moss Cataract, where, hesitating a moment on the brink, it dashes away over its mossy bed, fills Diana's bath* afresh, gives a leap over the falls of its own name, and hastens on to the Kittatinny to welcome the newly arrived guest, and after performing its office in the culinary department, takes a final leap of a hundred feet into the river.

* This place has been generally known as "*Venus's Bath*," but the original and more appropriate name is *Diana*, and as such will hereafter be known.

Cooper's Cliff.

For a morning, or after dinner walk, you pass through the gate in front of the hotel, and follow up Caldeno Creek, and notice as your guide the *white lines* on every suitable rock and tree. A walk of a few minutes along the stream brings you to the third geological step, to witness the surrounding hills mirrored in the bosom of a miniature lake, partly natural and partly artificial, known as "Lake Lenape." Turning from the lake to the left, still following the white lines, along a well-defined road, a distance of about one hundred yards, you observe a path to the right leaving yours at an acute angle, as if receding, only however to make the zigzag course up the precipitous eminence more easy of ascent. Follow this path and do not say it looks too tiresome, but save your breath till you reach "Cooper's Cliff," for when you are once there, you will have only enough left to exclaim, "How beautiful!"

Table Rock.

This is the fourth of the series of geological steps, or rather it is the commencement of an extended plateau of nearly horizontal rock, dipping slightly to the northwest, and composed of red shale, not inaptly called "Table Rock," and reaching for several miles along the base of Mount Minsi, cut in twain by the passage of Caldeno Creek at Moss Cataract. Cooper's Cliff is about three hundred feet in elevation above the hotel, and five hundred feet above the river. You will not be in a hurry to leave this spot. Up the river the view is varied and beautiful. The sweeping curve of the mountain; the green fields cultivated on the sides of the corresponding hills; the islands, and the river so closely hemmed in by hill and mountain as to resemble a lake, make altogether a picture of rare beauty. The most distant of these clearings, and covering the summit of Shawnee Hill, is Transue's Knob. Looking south, you have a fine, though *incomplete* view of the Gap, as the inevitable Blockhead Mountain still obstructs the view. Continue on the eastern edge of this plateau, following the white lines, as before indicated, and a walk of a few hundred yards over a mossy bed, brings you to that portion of Table Rock commanding a favorite view of the Gap.

The whole scene about this spot is picturesque. The confused mixture of forest and hills and cultivated land below the cliff on which you stand, form a beautiful foreground to the finely-developed proportions of the gorge in the distant mountain. The tall trees at the base of the cliff present no obstruction to the view, being far beneath the elevation on which you stand. The quiet little meadow looks as though it had been brought hither, and not made from the clearings of the forest surrounding it. It had not always this tame appearance, however; not many years ago it was a dense thicket, so filled with trees and wild bramble as to be almost impenetrable, and was a famous resort for catamount, and other wild animals then infesting the neighborhood. The father of the writer once killed at this place a catamount of unusual size and ferocity. Being armed with only a small hand axe, and accompanied by his dog, the latter was attacked and soon laid prostrate. Just as the beast was springing forward, the axe was thrown with such force and precision as to disable him, so that he was easily dispatched with a club.

Moss Cataract—Diana's Bath—Caldeno Falls.

A few hundred yards further on in the same general direction, and guided by the white lines, will bring you again to Caldeno Creek,—wilder now than when you last saw it near the hotel, because *farther in the woods,* and livelier because it has *more room to play.* When you are fairly down by the stream, if you had not seen the well-worn path leading to it, you would almost undertake to say no one had ever been here before you; so untouched is this picture by the hand of man, so perfectly is the whole in keeping with the harmony of nature. Moss Cataract, Diana's Bath, and Caldeno Falls, are all found in this wild ravine, and near each other.

Moss Cataract is a slide, or rather a tumble which the stream indulges in, of about a hundred feet in length, down the slope of Table Rock, at an angle of about forty-five degrees. This smooth rocky bed is covered with a thick green moss, not so abundant now as formerly, as frequent depredations are committed upon it by its fair visitors. The ravine is hemmed in by a thick growth of rhododendrons, and beyond these by tall trees, so that the sun never shines upon Diana either in her morning, evening, or noonday ablutions.

In the centre of this slide, nature has carved out of the solid rock* this little basin for her favorite goddess. Was ever nymph so honored? "You feel like taking a bath yourself?" Don't you do it. Diana's retinue of nymphs—whom you know were all sworn to celibacy, and by this time are very ancient, and perhaps surly maidens, may be secreted in the thick wood, keeping watch over the sacred precincts, with bow ready drawn, to execute the full measure of their wrath against you for such a desecration.

* This basin has somewhat the appearance of having been made by the hands of men, but *such is not the case.* It is known to have existed in its present form, long before the place was resorted to by visitors from the city.

Caldeno Falls makes the third of these gems of the romantic. The Falls are not like those of Niagara—*not quite so much.* And this reminds me of an equally profound remark of a lady traveller: "What a most wonderful place would be the Delaware Water Gap, *if Niagara Falls were here.*"

Caldeno received its title in 1851, by using syllables from the names of the three following gentlemen, who then visited it:

C. L. Pas-cal
C. S. Og-den
Jos. McD o-ud.*

From a spot so entirely secluded, so cool and pleasant, and so picturesque, you part with reluctance. You can return by the path from the Falls, and reach Table Rock at a lower point than that by which you entered this place, and can vary your route home by going directly across Table Rock, descend the cliff by an easy grade, and take the road through the little meadow, which leads you direct to the Kittatinny House.

* See letter from Mr. C. L. Pascal, at end of book.

Lover's Leap.

Leaving the hotel in the same direction as in the route to Caldeno Falls, and after ascending the first rise in front by Caldeno Creek, you turn to the left, and observe the stones and trees in this direction marked *Red.* You enter the woods in the rear of the bowling saloon, by an open road, and after a short but precipitous ascent, you gain the second elevation, and intersect a wagon road. This is not a *highway* in the general acceptation of the word, but in gaining some of the elevations reached by it, you will think it certainly entitled to that appellation. You have now a pleasant level walk of some distance, sheltered from the rays of the sun by tall trees, and skirted by a thick growth of laurel and rhododendron. Just before entering the little meadow seen from Table Rock, you pass the Cottage *d'Africaines.* Proceeding through the meadow, you gain another elevation, and have another level walk of some distance, sheltered and skirted as before, until you reach the path to the left, leading to "Lover's

Leap," marked at the entrance with blue. Besides the romance connected with the spot, you will pronounce Lover's Leap worthy of more than one visit. The view of the Gap from this point differs from any you have witnessed, and is the place selected by artists as affording the finest picture. That peculiar sweep in the river is seen to great advantage, as well as the corresponding curve in the mountain on the Pennsylvania side. Could "Winona," the *Indian Princess*, who, tradition says, once stood where we are now standing, have witnessed the train of cars as it emerges from behind the mountain in the Gap, she would readily have imagined it a messenger of destruction from some cavernous vault—an infernal region—deep in the bowels of the mountain, and fired up by the fiends inhabiting the dismal abode, and that it had been sent forth to devastate and depopulate the earth's surface.

It will be perceived that the spot selected by Winona for the execution of the fatal "leap," is not so favorable as some others near, as for instance, Prospect Rock; but as Winona, being the most interested party, saw fit—perhaps in her great haste,—to immortalize the place, we have no discretion in the matter. But more of Winona hereafter. We will now continue our rambles, and have the story of Lover's Leap when we have finished them.

The Hunter's Spring.

You will now retrace the pathway from Lover's Leap to the point of intersection with the road, and follow the *red lines.* A walk of half a mile brings you opposite "The Hunter's Spring." Now follow the *white lines* on a path leading to the right, and in a few rods' walk from the road, you reach this wild secluded spot, where many a "Lenape" huntsman, as well as those of modern times have been refreshed, and have lain in wait for the deer as they came panting for the cooling waters. The Hunter's Spring is the source of the rivulet that has its turbulent course down the mountain to the river, and which gives to the romantic ravine its life and beauty.

Prospect Rock.

At the road opposite the Hunter's Spring you take the direction of the *red* lines, as before, and enter the first path bearing to the left, and observe the *yellow lines* indicating the direction to *Prospect Rock*, which is gained by a pretty steep but not difficult walk of about four hundred yards. This bare platform, though still much below the summit of the Blue Ridge, of which it is a plication, enables the visitor to enjoy one of the finest views of the Delaware. The prospect up the river extends beyond the islands to the distant hills, and the mountain, through which the river winds its devious way, and then glides smoothly along the base of the almost perpendicular cliff from which you are gazing.

In the middle ground of this scene stands the Hotel and its surroundings, apparently as much below as beyond you.

The guests of the house remaining behind, are distinctly seen from the river balcony, waving signals in response to yours indicating your safe arrival at Prospect Rock.

Summit of Mount Minsi.

After you have sufficiently rested at Prospect Rock, proceed in the direction of the *red lines*, and do not be persuaded that the ascent to the Summit is too difficult. Hundreds of ladies and gentlemen have gone before you, and few have regretted the undertaking.

The journey is somewhat tiresome, and at places a little difficult; but, by resting occasionally, it can be overcome without great fatigue. The distance to the Summit is about one mile from Prospect Rock, and three miles from the Hotel.

This portion of the Kittatinny is named "Mount Minsi," from a particular branch of the Lenape Indians inhabiting the "Minisink country" (valley of the Delaware, north of the mountain). It is difficult to do full justice to a description of this view. It must be seen to be appreciated. You overlook an extent of country to the south as far as the eye can reach, a scene composed of mountains and hills in New Jersey and Pennsylvania, villages and farm-houses, cultivated fields, groves of woodland, and primitive forests; the river in its sinuous journey filling up the picture.

Sappers and Miners.

The Summit is also known as "Sappers' View," so named by a party of gentlemen organized many years ago under the title of "Sappers and Miners," and who until the last year or two, made the annual ascent to the "Summit," placing the dear old flag on the hightest tree to be seen from the Hotel, as well as one on the Summit. The view on the north side of the mountain is called "Miners' View." The object of the organization was primarily to open up some places of interest, not before easily accessible; and to honor "The Flag," by displaying its folds from the highest tree on the most elevated peak of the Kittatinny. The annual gathering increased in numbers and in interest, and the result has been, that under the protection of the Sappers and Miners, hundreds of ladies and gentlemen have visited "Mount Minsi," who would otherwise not have undertaken the journey, and thereby missed one of the finest views in the country.

Of the first organization we have no record. The first appearing on the Hotel Register is in 1858. Previous to this, it consisted of some eight or ten members, but when the last annual ascent was made, the number present had increased to seventy-five. The *officers*, from first to last, ranking from *general* to *high private* in the *military list;* and from "Historiographer" to "Pioneer" on the *civil list*, number about one hundred.

A sufficient number of ladies accompanying the expedition, usually remain with the commissary at the Hunter's Spring, to have the dinner, to be partaken of there, arranged in a manner suitable to this important anniversary, and in time for the return of the main party from the Summit.

After the repast, an hour or two is spent in patriotic speeches and songs, when the annual election of officers, presenting of badges, &c., take place.

The following is the list of officers who have at one time or another served in the organization, excepting those whose initials merely are given:

Gen. J. M. Vance,
William J. McElroy,
F. Gulager,
John Siner,
J. R. Chandler,
Robert Staley,
J. R. Field,
Morton McMichael, Jr.,
S. M. Lewis,
A. Engle,
Philip H. White,
W. R. Overman,
H. S. Davis,
A. M. Burton,
E. H. Saunders,
J. Bassett, Jr.,
George H. Brodhead,
W. H. Eisenbrey,
W. B. Knowles,
A. B Burrell,
William Murphey,
C. A. Jenks,
L. M. Bond, Jr.,
M. Abbott,
F. Maben,
H. B. Benners,
R. Dubois,
J. Dubois,
Mr. Lee,
W. H. Davis,
William Field,
Samuel Williams,
Rev. Mr. Wall,
Mr. Clarke,
W. M. Hodges,
M. Poillion,
G. Baker,
William Leveridge,
C. D'Invilliers,
J. D. Orton,
Dr. Bond,
Dr. Allen,
Rev. Mr. Edwards,
E. M. Benson,
Thomas E. Bacon,
William McMichael,
L. Godey,
G. W. Russell,
G. L. Harrison,
F. A. Drexel,
P. Ludlam,
J. Ogden,
J. S. Taylor,
Arthur Pike,
Edward L. Brodhead,
Jos. Wayne,
Loring Andrews, Jr.,
M. Sommerville,
L. C. Simon,
T. B. Belfield,
David Birch,
A. A. Hurley,
H. R. Raiguel,
S. B. Ely,
S. A. Stearns,
Rev. Mr. Cain,
S. P. Godwin,
H. Kershaw,
F. C. Hunnis,
H. Heberton,
M. Nagle,
Mr. Budd,
Dr. Dunscomb,
M. Masters,
Thomas McLean,
William McDaniels,
Dr. Ellis,
Joseph Siner.

The Rebellion interrupted somewhat the regular gathering of this ancient and honorable organization; and some of the young gentlemen who saluted our national emblem on the heights of Mount Minsi, have since honored themselves in its defence against rebels and traitors.

Gaps in the Kittatinny Mountain.

There are five depressions in the mountain, called "Gaps," between the Delaware Water Gap and the Lehigh Water Gap, over which wagon-roads pass, and from all of which fine views of the country on both sides of the mountain are to be had, viz.: Tatamy's Gap, Fox Gap, Wind Gap, Smith's Gap, and Little Gap, and distant from the Delaware Water Gap, respectively, in the order named: 2½ miles, 5 miles, 11 miles, 18 miles, 23 miles; and the Lehigh Water Gap, 29 miles. This is estimating in a direct line on the mountain from one Gap to the other. Tatamy's Gap was named after the Indian family of Tatamy's living south of the mountain. Moses Funda Tatamy or

Tetamy, was an interpreter for the Rev. John Brainerd, the faithful and zealous missionary among the Indians.*

The late M. S. Henry, in a letter to Dr. Brainerd, author of Life of John Brainerd, says: "The path or road over which Mr. Brainerd passed was the general thoroughfare from Philadelphia to Albany, the nearest route between those cities, and much frequented by travellers. The path (*road*, 'the old mine road'), commenced at or near Kingston, thence up the Esopus Creek, and down the Mackemack (Neversink) Creek to the river Delaware, which it crossed seven miles above Milford, in Pike County, Pa., and continued westwardly along the Blue Mountain to near the Delaware Water Gap, thence to the Lehigh Water Gap (through Cherry Valley), and thence in a nearly southwardly course to Philadelphia."

Brainerd had a missionary station at what

* Brainerd visited the Indians in the Minisink in 1743, and, at that time, none of the "Gaps" appear to have been considered passable by men on horseback, excepting the Lehigh Gap, and he went the whole distance of Cherry Valley (30 miles) to reach that point on his way to the "Forks," where Easton now stands.

is now known as "Allen's Ferry," seven miles below the Gap on the Delaware. The Indian town there was called "Sakauwatung," meaning "the mouth of a creek where some one resides." There was another Indian town, called "Clistowacki," meaning "fine land," where Brainerd built a cottage and lived for a time. It was situated near "the three brick churches," in Mount Bethel township, near the residence of Mr. Baker, and fifteen miles south of the Delaware Water Gap. A party of ladies and gentlemen, with the writer, visited the place last autumn, and obtained information relating to it from persons living there; and in the surrounding fields picked up a number of Indian relics of the stone age. The Indian burial-ground is near one of the churches.

I have before me an article from the "Easton Journal," giving an account of the closing career of "Tattamy Tundy" (a confusion of names, meaning, no doubt, Moses Funda Tatamy), an extract from which is as follows:

"When the Mohicans set out on their pilgrimage towards the setting of the sun, a lone warrior lingered behind. His affections were so riveted to the land of his nativity that he found it utterly impossible to abandon it. He resolved to remain: 'The last rose of summer, left blooming alone.' The proprietaries, or their agents, probably operated upon by a sense of the injustice they had done his tribe, suffered him to occupy a favorite spot on the Lehicton Creek, near the present village of Stockertown. Here he erected his wigwam, and for many years after the departure of his tribe, Tattamy Tundy might be seen stealing along the banks of the Lehicton, or sitting before his wigwam and humming the wild war-songs of his ancestors.

"At the breaking out of the Revolutionary War, the hostile Indians made frequent inroads upon the frontier settlements, and a change of residence was deemed necessary to secure the personal safety of Tattamy. He was removed to Frenchtown, on the Delaware. There he was permitted to occupy a small tract of land, and there he yielded up his spirit, near the close of the Revolutionary War."

Heckewelder speaks of "Tattemi," a beloved chief of the Delawares, as having been murdered at the Forks (Easton), about the year 1750, "by a foolish young man." He was succeeded by Tedeuskund.

See, also, Journal of Moses Titamy to the Minisink, Penna. Archives, vol. iii, p. 504, who also acted as interpreter. There were probably two or three distinguished persons of the same name,—brothers, and sons of William Tatamy. The father is probably the "chief" who was killed at Easton.

Smith's Gap is the one through which the party passed in the famous Indian walk.

Mount Tammany.

Mount Tammany,* the New Jersey summit of the Kittatinny, commands a view

* Mount Tammany was named after the distinguished Indian chief *Tamanend*, of whom Heckewelder says: "Of all the chiefs and great men which the Lenape nation ever had, he stands foremost on the list. But although many fabulous stories are circulated about him among the whites, but little of his real history is known. The misfortunes which have befallen some of the most beloved and esteemed personages among the Indians, since the Europeans came among them, prevented the survivors from indulging in the pleasure of recalling to mind the memory of their virtues. No white

similar to that witnessed from Mount Minsi. It is more difficult of ascent, but less broad on the top, and, therefore, enables you to look in all directions, excepting in range with the mountain. The ascent is made from the carriage-road along the river, near the slate factory in the Gap. The "Indian Ladder" was not, as is supposed by some, a

man, who regards their feelings, will introduce such subjects in conversation with them.

"All we know, therefore, of Tamanend is, that he was an ancient Delaware chief, who never had his equal. He was in the highest degree endowed with wisdom, virtue, prudence, charity, affability, meekness, hospitality, in short with every good and noble qualification that a human being may possess. . . . . In the Revolutionary War, his enthusiastic admirers dubbed him a saint, and he was established, under the name of *St. Tammany*, the patron saint of America. His name was inserted in some calendars, and his festival celebrated on the first day of May in each year. On that day, a numerous society of his votaries walked the streets of Philadelphia, their hats decorated with bucks' tails, and proceeded to a handsome rural place out of town, which they called the *Wigwam*, where, after a *long talk* or Indian speech had been delivered, and the *calumet* of peace and friendship had been duly smoked, they spent the day in festivities and mirth. . . . .

"Since that time, other societies have been formed in Philadelphia and New York, and in other towns in the Union, under the name of Tammany; but the principal object of these associations being party politics, they have lost much of the charm which was attached to the original society of St. Tammany."

series of steps up the side of the mountain to the summit, but merely a passage up and over the high sharp projection near the base of the mountain, in the line of the Indian path,—a sort of *promontory*, extending into the river, terminating in an acute angle. The ascent and descent, on the north side of this promontory, was by steps or footholds in the rocks, broken out, probably, by stone-mauls; and on the south side, which was more precipitous, by climbing a tree with the branches remaining on it, placed against the sloping side of this projection. After the path became more frequented by the early settlers, a wooden ladder was constructed in place of the tree used by the Indians. The present wagon-road was cut through this rocky promontory, and has left no traces of the "Indian Ladder."

Sunset Hill.

Whatever may have caused the wild disorder existing in and about these mountains, the varied and irregular appearance of the strata—at one place dislocated from upheavals, at another, only a few rods distant, regular and horizontal—will ever continue to be an inexhaustible field for the researches of the inquiring geologist.

> "Crags, knolls, and mounds, in dire confusion hurled,
> The fragmentary elements of an earlier world."

The exposed stratum of the bluff upon which the Hotel is situated, is broken, but nearly uniform; the next elevation immediately in the rear of the Hotel, is entirely horizontal, and to all appearance as undisturbed as when the plastic mass emerged from beneath the quiet waters, where by the slowly dropping sediment of untold ages, it had grown to its present proportions.

Only a few rods to the east of these undisturbed layers, Sunset Hill rises high above them, and is a confused, disjointed, irregular mass of rock from base to apex.

The dip of the exposed strata, both to the north and south from the summit, is at an angle corresponding with the varying declination of its surface.

From this spot, so interesting in its geological structure, is a view composed of all the varieties nature makes use of, in forming a landscape pleasing to the eye. To the south the proportions of the Gap are well defined, and from this point Mr. Darley, the artist, delighted most to behold it. Looking to the north and east, you trace the waving outlines of the Shawnee Hills, the long stretch of the Kittatinny, and the lake-like repose of the Delaware, with the lower portion of Cherry Valley and the village in the nearer view. You will be disappointed in going to see the sun set from this hill, and will conclude there is a misapplication of the name, as the last rays of the sun are obstructed by the grove of trees to the west. But the pleasure to be enjoyed at this hour of the day, and in which the name has its significance, is to witness the shadows made from the waving outline of hills to the west, as they slowly climb the side of the mountain, rising higher and higher as the "dying orb" sinks to the horizon.

Sunset Hill is the site selected for the contemplated hotel. We hope ere long to see it stand forth in proportions corresponding to the grandeur of the situation; the additional view of Cherry Valley obtained from the upper balconies, will make the prospect altogether one of the finest to be witnessed from any hotel in the Union.

Mount Caroline.

Following up the carriage-road in the direction of the village until you come to the little "Church of the Mountain," and on an elongated cone immediately in the rear of the church, you have an extended view of rare beauty, and if your stay at the "Gap" is long, you will visit it again and again. To the west you have a beautiful view of the lower portion of Cherry Valley, and the creek lazily winding through it, as if lingering in this lap of loveliness before losing its identity in the waters of the Delaware. To the northwest is a long stretch of undulating hill, commencing some ten miles up Cherry Valley, known as "Fox Hill," and skirting its border, abruptly cut asunder by the passage of Brodhead's Creek, rising immediately on the opposite bank, forming a high coniform bluff, named "Mount Lewis." The range of hill from the creek to its connection with the Kittatinny, some twelve miles further northeast, is called "Shawnee Hill."

Passing the village of Shawnee, and affording a resting-place there in one of its depressions for the dead of more than a century, it rises to its apex at Transue's Knob, and soon after is lost to view from Mount Caroline. As the eye follows down the Delaware, it takes in the Islands, Indian Hill, and down at the base of the cliff, the village of the Water Gap.

This place, so unmeaningly named heretofore, shall be called hereafter "Mount Caroline," after a lady who has long admired it, and who for twenty-eight consecutive seasons has honored the Delaware Water Gap with her presence. It is the more appropriate too, as the little church, so quietly nestled in these hills, has ever been to her an object of tender solicitude.

Laurel Hill.

Laurel Hill stands immediately in front of Mount Caroline. The view from this point is similar to the other, though not so extended; but during the month of June, when the laurel is in bloom, it is much frequented, and much admired by the early visitors at the Gap.

Blockhead Mountain.

Blockhead Mountain is a spur of the Blue Ridge on the New Jersey side of the river, branching out from the main mountain a few miles above, and terminating abruptly opposite the inner curve of the Pennsylvania Mountain, in range with Prospect Rock, with which it was no doubt at one time connected, and formed the first barrier to the passage of the river. Nobody seems to know when Blockhead Mountain received its name, or why it was so named. It is no great favorite, and there seems to be not much respect entertained for his *Highness*, though it be sufficiently elevated to shut out the view of the Gap from the Hotel.

The complaint of those who are obliged to remain at the house who cannot climb the hills for a better view, is, that they may look at the Gap as they will, and contemplate it as they may, Blockhead Mountain is sure to have its *foot* in it. Notwithstanding these complaints, it is not without interest. The serpentine course of the river in its passage through the mountains, is "Blockhead's" doings, and adds very much to the beauty of the scene as witnessed from the carriage-road at Rebecca's Bath, or from a boat on the water. Blockhead Mountain also commands a very fine view of the Gap from its summit.

Lovers' Retreat, or the Haunted Pine.

On the second plateau, the first from the Hotel, and on a rise of one hundred feet from the latter, and only a few rods south of the Bowling Saloon, long years beyond the recollection of the oldest, and until within the memory of the younger, there stood on the edge of the precipice, with his roots sunk deep in the crevices of the rocks, among smaller and less important trees, *an aged pine.*

The place where it stood was one of the earliest, and still is one of the most favorite near resorts, especially for lovers; perhaps, because it can only be approached from one direction, and affords no opportunity for sudden surprisals. The old tree is dead now, and "the place that once knew it, will know it no more," excepting in its spectral apparitions. And of it we might sing, as of the lamented "Grimes:"

> "Th' old pine is dead, that dear old tree,
> We ne'er shall see it more;
> It used to wear that old green coat,
> So often worn before."

But, as old pines outlive everything about them (who ever heard of one dying from natural causes?) it was thought proper that an inquiry should be instituted to ascertain, if possible, the cause of its premature dissolution. On examination, it was found that the willing soil still yielded nourishment to its thrifty survivors, that the canker-worm had not penetrated its vitals, that it had received no rude cuttings by the hands of the thoughtless axeman, nor in fact any apparent injury; but after a long and thoughtful, and ponderous meditation, the committee returned with the stunning verdict, "that the tree came to its death from the effects of *heat, engendered by the too ardent appeals of importunate suitors.*" Nobody, of course, gave any credence to such a report; but shortly after, on a bright moonlight night, when at the Hotel there was mirth and gayety,

> "And all went merry as a marriage bell,"

the startling alarm was given, and the "old pine" was seen to be on *fire*, and as the flames ascended high up in the air and illumined the whole cliff, a *pair of lovers* were seen quietly to emerge from the place and make their descent toward the Hotel, upon which a member of the committee, who happened to be present, had the temerity to make the ungallant remark, that, "now the truth of their verdict was *more* than confirmed." Since then the place is reported to be *haunted*; and haunted it is, if ever a spot was haunted; and why may not ghosts inhabit the *body of a tree* as well as *anybody else?* Vague and uncertain sounds are heard to issue from the place even on moonlight evenings, in tones from a gentle whisper to plaintive lamentations.

Martin's Rest.

On the carriage-road leading north from the Hotel, and as it turns the point at the base of Sunset Hill, there is a view very similar to that seen from its summit, heretofore described.

A few steps up the side of the hill a seat is erected, on which may be seen on many a warm summer evening, a party long and pleasantly remembered by many a sojourner at the Kittatinny House. The place is known as "Martin's Rest."

Church of the Mountain.

The church is a few minutes' walk from the Hotel. It was built both for the accommodation of the visitors at the Gap, and the people of the neighborhood, liberal contributions having been made for that purpose by those who, more or less frequently, visit this place.* Previous to its erection, the

* For the conception and successful prosecution of this design, all who feel an interest in the little Church of the Mountain, will hold in grateful remembrance the names of Mrs. Franklin Peale and Dr. J. Marshall Paul.

nearest churches were at Stroudsburg and Shawnee. But the zealous and indefatigable Methodists embraced this in their field of Christian labor, and worshipped in the schoolhouse and in private families almost since the village had existence. Twenty-five years ago extra meetings were held, at suitable seasons of the year, in my father's barn. Many pleasant recollections of boyhood days are associated with the weekly or semi-monthly visits of the youthful itinerant preachers, who, like the schoolmasters of former days, "boarded 'round," and, to each family in turn, were always welcome guests.

The church was erected in 1854, and was dedicated in the month of July of that year. The Rev. Horatio S. Howell was the first pastor. He came to the Water Gap in August, 1853, and organized the church (New School Presbyterian) the following winter. Mr. Howell continued as pastor until March, 1862, when he was chosen chaplain of the Ninetieth Regiment Pennsylvania Volunteers, commanded by Colonel Lyle, and was killed by a rebel soldier whilst attending to the sick and wounded at the Hospital in Gettysburg, July 1st, 1863. The following report of this melancholy event was made by a correspondent of one of the city papers at the time:

"DOWNRIGHT MURDER.

"On the afternoon of the 1st, as the rebels charged through the town, the pistols carried by them, and with which they had been abundantly supplied, were fired promiscuously at all who might be in the street, looking out of windows, or standing in the doorways.

"A squadron of this charging party rode directly up to the front of the hospital and deliberately discharged their pistols at those who were standing upon the steps and upon the walks in front. This firing instantly robbed our service of one of its most pious, excellent, and beloved chaplains, the Rev. Mr. Howell, of the Ninetieth Pennsylvania Regiment."

Mr. Howell's death cast a gloom over the entire neighborhood. He was, indeed, a most beloved pastor, a noble, generous-hearted man, and an ardent patriot.

The Rev. E. J. Pierce was the successor of Mr. Howell. The present pastor, Rev. S. W. Knipe entered upon his labors in May of this year.

The following extract from the sermon delivered at the dedication of the Church of the Mountain will be interesting to most persons who visit this place:

DEDICATION SERMON,

CHURCH OF THE MOUNTAIN, DELAWARE WATER GAP, PENNSYLVANIA.

BY THE REV. F. F. ELLINWOOD,
Pastor of the Second Presbyterian Church, Belvidere, N. J.

AUGUST 29, 1854.

"THUS SAITH THE LORD OF HOSTS, CONSIDER YOUR WAYS; GO UP TO THE MOUNTAIN AND BRING WOOD, AND BUILD THE HOUSE, AND I WILL TAKE PLEASURE IN IT, AND I WILL BE GLORIFIED, SAITH THE LORD."—*Haggai* 1 : 7, 8.

For many centuries past, has Jehovah dwelt in the rocky fastnesses of this mountain. Ere there was a human ear to listen, His voice was uttered here in the sighing of the breeze and the thunder of the storms, which even then were wont to writhe in the close grapple of this narrow gorge. Ere one human footstep had invaded the wildness of the place, or the hand of art had applied the drill and blast to the silent rock, God's hand was working here alone—delving out its deep, rugged pathway for yonder river, and clothing those gigantic bluffs and terraces with undying verdure, and the far-gleaming brightness of their laurel bloom. Every day since that first dawn whereat the morning stars sang joyfully together, has God been present here, in Nature's *broad temple*, which, as the ancient Germani would tell us, is alone *adequate* to the indwelling of the Infinite One; but never, until *this* day, has He dwelt here in a temple made with hands.

Never, amid these almost eternal rocks, has an event like this to-day transpired before. We trust that, for years past, there have been individual hearts in which the presence of God has here been felt, and we know not but earlier still, the Red man, catching, it may be, the name of Jesus from the lips of the beloved Brainerd, has tuned here in wild notes the songs of Zion; or, on this very spot, kneeling at the calm sunset hour, has breathed the prayer of a renewed heart to heaven. But not until this day have God's people here thrown open the doors of a consecrated temple, and sat down therein, to wait in prayerfulness together, while the unseen Jehovah—heavenly guest —should come and make His dwelling in their midst. Thus sit we here together now. The temple has been built; all things are ready, and what wait we for but the presence of our God? "Lift up your heads, O! ye gates, and be ye lifted up ye everlasting doors, and the King of Glory shall come in. Who is this King of Glory? The Lord, strong and mighty; the Lord, mighty in battle. Lift up your heads, O! ye gates; even lift them up ye everlasting doors, and the King of Glory shall come in. Who is this King of glory? The Lord of Hosts, He is the King of Glory."

The present occasion may well be one of great rejoicing to us all, my friends, since to-day a fond hope is realized. It seems but yesterday that we assembled here, in the open air, to lay the corner-stone of this edifice; and while the sultry autumnal sun was beaming warm upon us, and the solemn, yet beautiful October tinge was dappling all these wooded heights, we stood with uncovered heads and commended this unbuilt temple to the care of Almighty God—feeling as the Psalmist felt, that "except the Lord build the house, they do labor in vain that build it." But now we meet to rejoice, with thanksgiving, that our prayer has been heard; that God's blessing has rested upon this holy enterprise, and that we are here permitted to sit in those heaven-appointed courts, wherein one day, rightly spent, is better than a thousand in the tents of wickedness. It seems but yesterday, too, that wintry day on which we met in the small school-house opposite, and organized a church who should thenceforth worship God in this mountain, and felt that the place was too strait for those who had assembled, and looked forward with hope to the time when we should meet in God's own house. That hope is now realized to the full extent: we find its fruition in the pleasantness and convenience of this beautiful structure. "How amiable are thy Tabernacles, O Lord of Hosts! Blessed are they that dwell in thy house; they shall be still praising thee!"

It is an interesting feature in the objects of this occasion, that the result which we here behold is but the consummation of a purpose which God himself had long since formed. It was He who, by one means or another, first said to his people, with reference to this work, "Go up to the mountain, and bring wood and build the house, and I will take pleasure in it, and I will be glorified, saith the Lord." It was He who, by the leadings of his Providence and the influence of his Spirit, first put it into the heart of a Christian woman to devise and commence this noble work. It was He who raised up other promoters of his kingdom, who, with responsive and willing hearts, took up and carried forward what had been commenced. It was He who called forth the prayers and efforts of his children in this place; for, as in the days of Nehemiah, so here "the people had a mind to work," and "all the wall was joined together." It was God primarily who planned it all, and to Him the sincere thanks of every heart are due. Indeed, He has been preparing for this church during many years and even ages past. There is not a beam in all this edifice but He reared it for the very purpose which it here subserves—even when its germ first rooted in the mould of the mountain side; He saw the object of its existence in the building of this house. Neither is there a stone in the edifice which He did not prepare for its present use; and as to the firm foundation whereon this structure rests, God said of it, ages ago, as He did of Peter, "On this rock I will build my church." That fiat is this day brought to complete execution. The rude blasts of six thousand winters have howled in undaunted wildness over the consecrated spot, while yet its predicted destiny was not fulfilled; but here, at length, stands, in very deed *the church firmly built* upon the rock, and it is our hope and prayer that the gates of hell shall not prevail against it.

But we turn from the past to the future. You have been up to the mountain, and brought wood, and built the house, led on, as we verily believe, by the eternal design and moving power of God; you have been sanctioned, we trust, and blest by Him in all the work from first to last, and therefore by implication we may plead His promise, that He will take pleasure in this built and dedicated Temple, and be glorified therein. Even in the planning and building of the church, though nothing further should be done, though by some casualty this edifice should be now destroyed, even in that which has been already accomplished, God is glorified, and yet we would feel that his greatest glory in this church will be derived from that which in future shall here be done. We would regard the temple itself as the means only to a greater end; we would look onward hopefully to the effectual and widespread working of God's Holy Spirit here; we would think of the multitudes who may hereafter receive the Word of Eternal Life in this consecrated place; we would anticipate the growth of a large and flourishing church and congregation here—one whose influence for good shall extend itself over all these mountains, and whose Heaven-reflected light shall shine out through all these valleys, so that spiritually, as well as literally, this may prove to be a city set upon a hill, which therefore cannot be hid. And we would rejoice in the thought that hereafter those from our cities, who shall resort to this mountain for health or pleasure, may here find health indeed, in the healing "balm of Life," and "pleasures for evermore," at the hand of God; that such of their number as love the gates of Zion at home, may here also find a sanctuary with its holy Sabbath service; while those who love not God—whom the business and pleasure and fashions of city life have kept ever whirling in the maelstrom of worldliness, may here, at least, in the quiet of this secluded temple, be brought for the first time to Christ, through the simple and earnest preaching of the Word.

And, my friends, it is a glorious hope which we indulge to-day, that never again, while time shall last, shall there be wanting in this mountain an abode for the living God; that although a hundred centuries more should be added to the unknown age of these solid rocks, they may never be found without at least one church. Indeed, when we reflect upon the progressive nature of the Redeemer's Kingdom, and at the same time the progressive tendencies of this country, now becoming, instead of China, the middle kingdom of the world, we see no reason to suppose that the time ever *will* come when no church will here be found. We have no fear of a retrograde movement, although such cases have indeed been known. We can conceive of and hope for great advancement here; we can look forward fifty years, and imagine four or five churches standing in the midst of a flourishing village; we can conceive of a time,—perhaps a century to come,—when a halo of historic interest shall have gathered round each name of the original assembly who dedicated the little antique church upon the hill,—when those who moved in building it shall be held in grateful honor, and when a leaf of the Dedication Sermon, if found, would be regarded as a quaint relic of a comparatively barbarous age. All this is perhaps supposable, but we expect no turning back—no abatement of interest; we hope for life and action and constant progress. We cannot resist the impression that we are honored of God to-day, in being permitted to begin a work which shall not end till all earthly things shall end, nor even then; and I would say for your encouragement, my friends, that with faithfulness on your part, in carrying out the holy enterprise which you have commenced, a thousand recipients of blessings here may rise up and call you blessed at the last great day. If here, both by your personal effort and your pecuniary means, you lend a liberal hand in maintaining the ordinances of grace; if here unitedly you watch and pray for souls, believing that God will answer; if here you instruct the young, training them from very childhood to labor in your places when you are gone, thus carrying on from generation to generation this glorious work; then how many, oh! how many precious stars for the Redeemer's crown will ultimately have been gathered in this place! How great a good will have been accomplished from this beginning!

From the preliminary points which have thus far been touched upon, it will readily be seen that much of God's glory in this church lies yet in the future, and is intimately connected with the degree of holy and earnest activity which his people here are expected to put forth in time to come. We see that when by His Providence he said to you, "Go up to the mountain and bring wood and build the house," and when He promised to take pleasure and be glorified therein, something was implied which yet remains for you to do. In directing you to build the house, the design with which it is built was kept constantly in view, of course. While, therefore, we have great reason to congratulate *you*, my friends, and render our heartfelt thanks to Heaven in view of that which already has been done, it becomes an interesting and profitable inquiry for us, and one appropriate to the occasion, how, so far as future effort is concerned, *may* God best be glorified in this newly-dedicated temple? Let this be the one prominent question, not only for this discourse and this occasion, but forever, so long as the church shall stand. How, according to the promise in our text, shall God best be glorified in this His own holy habitation?

CARRIAGE DRIVES.

THE places of interest in and about the Gap are divided into two classes: those seen by pedestrians, and of easy access from the Hotel, and those seen by carriage-drives of from three to fifteen miles. Of the latter class are Cherry Valley and Stroudsburg, with the intermediate view from Fox Hill, Cherry Valley, and Crystal Hill, Buttermilk Falls, Marshall's Falls, and Bushkill Falls, Shawnee Hill, Transue's Knob, Castle Rock, Slate Factories and Quarries, and the New Jersey hills. The summit of Mount Minsi can also be reached by a circuitous drive of some six miles; but as the road is rough and precipitous, this journey should be made on horseback, if not, on foot *via* Prospect Rock.

The roads to all these points, excepting the last named, are firm and comparatively smooth, but hilly; no one, however, who passes over them will wish the hills less elevated, or the valleys less deep, as the beauty of the scenery is much enhanced thereby.

Cherry Valley from Fox Hill.

Fox Hill, alluded to in the view from Mount Caroline, is elevated above the river from three hundred feet to five hundred feet, and its whole length, including the portion east of Brodhead's Creek, called Shawnee Hill, about twenty-five miles. It has its termination in the Kittatinny Mountain, a short distance from where the Delaware divides it, near Flat Brook in New Jersey.

At one of the depressions in Fox Hill, the carriage-road passes to Stroudsburg. Near the summit of the road, a portion of Cherry Valley is seen to the left, and so hemmed in with mountains you wonder where the quiet comfortable-looking inhabitants find their egress. The creek seems in no hurry to find an outlet, for after slowly wandering on its journey for some distance, it makes an irregular circuit, and returns to within a few rods of the place it left a little while before, and forms a considerable peninsula, resembling in appearance an exaggerated pedal member, called the "Giant's Foot." The whole scene is a picture of rural beauty, much admired by visitors.

Stroudsburg.

On the west side of Fox Hill, another valley of equal beauty with Cherry Valley, and of greater variety, is witnessed from the carriage-road. It is, like the former, nearly encircled with mountains and hills, the most distant and very prominent is a spur of the Pocono. It stands out like a grand monument, the lesser hills rising one above another from the valley, forming a substantial pedestal on which to rest its giant proportions. The town, of about two thousand inhabitants, is pleasantly situated in the lower portion of the valley of the Pocono. Three beautiful streams unite on its eastern border. It has a large extent of valley land to spread over, and when the cities of Philadelphia and New York are reached in a reasonable time by rail, it will afford inducements for the erection of country residences, equal to any situation on either thoroughfare.

On your return from Stroudsburg you cross Fox Hill at a point a short distance to the west, and have another and different view of Cherry Valley, and a pleasant ride through it to the Kittatinny House.

Cherry Valley and Crystal Hill.

Cherry Valley runs nearly parallel with the Kittatinny Mountain; the portion west of the Wilkesbarre turnpike to the Lehigh is called Achquonshicola, after the creek of that name, which flows west into the Lehigh above Lehigh Gap, having its rise near that of Cherry Creek, which flows in an opposite direction to the Delaware. The whole length of the valley being about thirty-five miles.

The usual distance of the drive is from seven to ten miles, and is full of interest and beauty. Crystal Hill requires a walk of half a mile from the valley road to its summit. The whole of the rocky surface is more or less crystalline, and some very fine specimens of quartz are sometimes obtained.

A short distance up the valley from here, in Shaw's meadows, are seen those conical hills of diluvial deposit, produced no doubt by the surging of the water and the action of fields of ice against the sides of the mountain at the time when the waters covering the valley of the Minisink were supposed to have had their elevated outlet at the Wind Gap, and before the bursting asunder of the mountain at the Water Gap.

Buttermilk Falls.

The ledge over which the creek passes at this point, is composed of fossiliferous limestone. Over these dark rocks the stream spreads in tortuous channels, through which it has worked its way in eccentric and even grotesque whirls. The water so fretted and chafed into foam is not unlike in appearance the homely product of the dairy, which has given its name to this unique cascade.

Buttermilk Falls and Marshall's Falls are on the same stream, and can both be seen in a morning's or after-dinner's ride. The distance to the first is three miles, and to Marshall's Falls seven miles. Their beauty depends much upon the condition of the stream, being greatly enhanced when the volume of water is increased.

Marshall's Falls.

The rocks of this vicinity are of a dark color, and are filled with fossil casts and impressions; they are seamed all over with fissures and cracks, so much so, as to be easily detached in irregular shaped fragments by the action of the elements. The skilful use of the hammer and chisel will reveal some fine specimens of the trilobites, ammonites, and bivalve shells. The waters of Marshall's Creek have worn their way through this ledge in a chasm of some fifty feet in depth, leaving an overhanging cliff on the right side of the spectator, from beneath which he gazes through a portal between the approaching rocks upon the cataract, which falls into an interior basin, inaccessible because filled with water, which, after its short and precipitous career over the rapids above, makes its final leap into the dark basin, and flows thence through the narrow portal above mentioned; thence expanded to a wider sheet, and finally in a rippling course takes its way towards the Delaware.

Bushkill Falls.

On the way to Bushkill Falls, and three miles from the hotel, you pass over a portion of the Shawnee Hill projecting from the main range. From this elevation is a fine prospect both up and down the river, and of the lower portion of Cherry Valley; a view embracing much that has heretofore been described, but now seen from a point so favorable as to give it additional beauty. At the foot of the hill you pass the village of Shawnee, where the first settlement north of the mountain was formed. The whole of the first ten miles of the road to Bushkill is along the river, through a well-cultivated valley, between the parallel range of mountain and hill, and adorned with pictures of rural beauty rarely equalled. At the end of this drive you leave the river road, and ascend the Shawnee Hill again. When near the summit, do not fail to climb the bluff, a short distance to the right of the road, named Florabunda.

From this point you overlook the valley through which you have just passed, including the narrow belt of cultivated land in New Jersey, so beautifully sloping from the base of the mountain to the river, called Pahaqualong. The settlement is contemporary with that at Shawnee.

A short distance below where the mountain approaches the river the ancient copper mines are situated. The view up the river is in contrast with that just witnessed. The stream, being closely hemmed in by mountain and hill, with a thickly wooded island in the centre, presents a wild forest-like appearance.

The bold sweep which the river makes to the Pennsylvania shore just below where you stand has carried away a large body of its alluvial banks. It is called by the lumberman "Loving Shore," the current of the stream giving the rafts a strong inclination in that direction.*

* It seems to be a fact, and if so, worthy of observation, that the banks on the Delaware River are more injured in times of high water on the western or Pennsylvania shore

Three miles from here you reach the town of Bushkill, pleasantly situated on the stream of the same name, and here is an inviting place to take a rest at a clean, comfortable Hotel, kept by Mr. Peters. By giving orders you will have an excellent dinner in readiness on your return from the "Falls."

A part of the remaining journey along the Bushkill Creek is picturesque. The latter portion is through a newly-settled country, and the road rough and hilly. After you have lost all signs of civilization and may, perhaps, be wondering whether

> "The sound of the church-going bell
> These valleys and rocks ever heard,"

you suddenly come upon a *church*, standing solitary and alone in the forest; and however much you may be interested in the good work of erecting temples of worship at every suitable place, you will wonder what

than on that of New Jersey, where the near approach of the mountain does not prevent it, the inclination of the current, in times of freshets, being more in that direction. What it takes from Pennsylvania, however, in alluvium, it gives back to New Jersey in diluvium, or cleanly washed sand and gravel, of which its citizens protest they have *quantum sufficit.*

extraordinary Christian zeal could have induced the building of a church out of sight, and out of sound, of human habitation or human worshipper; but here it is, with its sad accompaniment, a burial-ground, and its silent inhabitants

"Imploring the passing tribute of a sigh."

The Falls are a few rods' walk from the church. Nature has wrought very beautifully in this wild secluded spot; and yet, until quite recently, these Falls remained comparatively unknown. Shall we doubt, however, that the rude and uncultivated red men were sensible to their beauty; and that their wild notes of admiration were less ardent than our own encomiums? The chasm is surrounded on three sides by a nearly perpendicular wall of rock. On one of these walls opposite the Falls you stand to witness the stream as it emerges from the thick woods, and leaps over the precipice into the dark interior basin beneath where you stand. Whirled and chafed into a foam it passes into the narrow gorge below, and is lost to view by the overhanging rocks. The Falls are ninety-six feet in height, broken in the centre by the abrasion of the water on the upper portion of the cliff, which rather adds to than detracts from their beauty. But you are quite as much impressed with the adamantine chamber below you, and its wild surroundings, as with the Falls themselves.

On your return from Bushkill, take what is known as the "middle road," through a well-cultivated portion of high table-land, studded with substantial and comfortable-looking farm-houses.

Falls of Winona.

These Falls are situated on Saw Creek, a branch of the Bushkill, about eleven miles from the Water Gap.

They were unfrequented and almost unknown, except by those who occasionally resorted to the mountain stream for trout-fishing, until the summer of 1867, a party visited the place from the hotel.

The stream is wild and picturesque, and contains in the distance of two miles, six beautiful waterfalls, named respectively by the party then present, in their order as you follow up the stream: *Clinton, Twin, Marybright, Glen Martin, Winona*, and *Dancing Waters*. Of these, "Winona" is the largest, and was named by the ladies after the heroine of the legend of "Lover's Leap." It is difficult to conceive of a more charming and romantic series of pictures than is found in this wild secluded mountain glen.

Transue's Knob.

On the Shawnee Hill, six miles from the Hotel, there stands, a hundred feet above the limestone measure of which the hill is a component, a pyramidal deposit of diluvium, covering several acres, composed mainly of pebbles and coarse gravel. Whether this curious formation of the aqueous element is Noachian, or whether the waters of the Delaware for a time rose above its summit, and made eccentric gyrations around this spot, and deposited in the interior of the irregular circle this mass of drift, at the time when the body of water commenced to find an outlet at the Gap, it is impossible to determine; but it will always afford an interesting subject of inquiry to the geologist. From this bald summit there is a panoramic view of great extent and beauty. A blending of the wildest forest scenes with cultivated fields and scattered farm-houses.

The river lies spread out before you, calm and serene now, for its work is done. Nature's solid masonry having yielded, atom by atom, until the unceasing waters have found their wonted bed.

Castle Rock.

On what is called the middle road to Bushkill, about four miles from the Hotel, is Castle Rock. The strange and sometimes inexplicable forms of geological structure, of which this is a striking example, can only be realized by a visual examination. From the face of the steep slope of Shawnee Hill, the rocks project and overlook the valley through which the road passes, like a fortress of ancient days, to defend the pass. The name is sufficiently indicative, and quite appropriate.

New Jersey Hills.

This drive is a circuit of twelve miles. Passing the Gap you cross the river in a flat-boat three miles below, and return through the mountains on the opposite side of the river, having a fine view of the Gap on both sides above and below. The road follows the windings of the river and skirts the base of the mountain the whole distance; nearly opposite the Hotel you ascend the hills, and have a variety of pictures that you will admire and long retain pleasant recollections of. You recross the river at the ferry three miles above, and return home by the Shawnee Hills.

Lake of the Mountain.

This is a sheet of pure transparent water surrounded by an irregular curved outline of foliage, and clear bare fragments and masses of gray sandstone, strangely and unaccountably situated upon the very summit of the mountain on the New Jersey side of the river. A mirror of beauty in the solitary wilderness, three-quarters of a mile in length, and something less in breadth, reflecting the image of the clouds, the only objects above its fair surface, beneath which in its transparent depths, the perch roam in solitary and peaceful independence.

The lake is reached by a carriage-ride to the ferry at Shawnee, and then by a rugged mountain path, accessible to all who have stout limbs and good lungs, and desire to have these requisites of healthful existence continued.

Indian Relics.

The articles of the *stone age* found so plentifully in this valley were, no doubt, those made and used by the Indians last inhabiting it; and their abundance seems to be evidence of friendly intercourse with the whites, as they were known to abandon their own implements, and adopt at the first opportunity those better suited to their purpose, introduced by the Europeans. In other sections of the country, known to have been inhabited by Indians in large numbers, comparatively few articles of their own fabrication are to be found, showing that they left hurriedly, and took with them their own implements.

The number found in an extent of ten miles in this valley, of stone, bone, and terracotta, would appear incredible to relate to one unfamiliar with the locality.

The collection seen at the Hotel, comprising perhaps a thousand pieces, is probably not the one-hundredth part of the number obtained. It is to be regretted that we know so little, comparatively, of a people possessing many traits of character we cannot but admire, and who were so friendly to our ancestors,—until being dealt unjustly with were driven to seek revenge;—who were the admiring possessors of these beautiful mountains and valleys, and who are now entirely passed away, with no record, and scarcely a tradition of their doings remembered.

We know little, too, of their mode of burial—less of the ceremonials. They were not *mound builders*, like those of the Mississippi Valley, yet they appear to have made selection of elevated places, and invariably commanding a view of the water and valley.

The two cemeteries spoken of in this locality are remarkable for the beauty of scenery afforded.

All, however, were not deposited in regular burial-places, as single bodies are sometimes exhumed by the plough, and frequently washed out along the river-banks. Whether these were enemies, or those less respected, or what caused the discrimination, cannot be determined. Like all the race, they deposited with the dead, articles most highly prized by them whilst living.

In the construction of implements and tools they never advanced beyond what archæologists denominate the *stone age*.

In this period of man's progress, however, are included *bone* and *terra-cotta* or earthen-made articles. There has been but one article found in this valley, so far as known, that can be said to belong to the "*bronze age*." This was a *copper axe*, made however from the raw material, and ground down to the required size and form.

The stone utensils found in the Minisink consist of *agricultural implements*, *pestles* and *mortars*, *hand-mill stones*, *chisels*, *hammers*, *axes*, *flint knives*, *arrow-points*, *spear-heads*, *tomahawks*, *personal ornaments*, and *pipes*, and those belonging to the fictile art, consisting of *pots*, *vases*, *bowls*, *plates*, &c.

The articles of stone used for agricultural purposes are comparatively few in number. Those most evidently made with that design are circular slate discs, one-fourth of an inch in thickness, notched on opposite sides, and about the size of our broad hoe, and were probably used in the same way and for like purposes, with withe handles. For breaking up and loosening the soil, they used *wood* and *bone*. The *shoulder blade* of the *elk* and *buffalo* answered the purposes of the *plough* and *spade*. The *pestles* were used in stone and wooden *mortars*, for grinding or mashing corn, the preparation of medicines, &c. In size, they are from six inches to twenty-four inches in length, and from one and a half to three inches in diameter. The method of constructing the pestle is very satisfactorily described by the late lamented Franklin Peale, of Philadelphia, in a communication read before the American Philosophical Society.

The process of "pecking" and rubbing or grinding applies to almost all the stone-made articles, excepting the spear-head, arrow-point, and flint knives. Mr. Peale says:

"A water-worn stone was selected, approximated by natural agency and action, the abrasion of moving masses in water, to the desired form. The superabundant material was then removed by a process which may be called 'pecking,' the characteristic marks of which appear upon a numerous class of instruments, such as pestles, mortars, chisels, &c. It was effected by blows with the sharp points of horn-stone, jasper, or chalcedony, either directly with a mass of those materials held in the hand, or aided by a mallet or club, or secured to wooden handles, by insertion and ligaments of tendon, or lashings of raw hide; the said blows were given in a direction perpendicular to the surface, and not with the tool placed at an angle, as is usual in chipping or dressing marble, thus strongly and plainly marking the surface of the larger and rougher implements, and more delicately those of the smaller or lesser.

"From the number of fragments found it is evident that many implements must have been broken under the operation. It is also evident from the numerons unfinished specimens found, that the characteristic unsustained labor of savages caused many to be abandoned with careless indifference in an unfinished state, after considerable time and work had been bestowed upon them.

"This manner of working off by crushing the surface is analogous in principle to the usages of modern 'stonecutters' when working upon sandstone and granite, but it is not adapted to marble, which requires that the tool should be held and struck at an angle (with this marked difference, that they use tools of steel), so as to lift off chips without crushing, and thus destroying the structure of the marble; by the first method noted, unskilful workmen destroy or greatly injure works of art.

"After the implement had been brought by *pecking* to the required form, a higher degree of finish was given by rubbing with sandstones, or by rubbing it upon sandstone rocks until the peck-marks were either partially or wholly obliterated, and the implement thus finished.

"It is evident that the higher degree of finish exhibited by the polish of some articles, was the result of a higher grade of workmanship, with materials properly selected, upon principles similar to those employed at the present day.

"The operation of *pecking* upon a detached rock confined to a circular space, enabled the patient laborer to work out a cavity capable of receiving a quantity of maize or other grain, and thus a mortar was made; not invariably, however, upon a detached mass, as they have been observed upon rocks in place.

"This method of working leaves a mark entirely dissimilar to any produced by natural causes. The rolling of floods has a tendency to remove the angles and corners of broken fragments detached from their beds by frost and water or other elemental causes. Changes of temperature are rounding and smoothing, or produce entire disintegration, but the mark made by the above-described means can never, when once observed, be mistaken for anything else than man's work, and the eye that has once carefully observed it will never fail in its recognition. It is also so with the conchoidal fracture of silicious implements, which unmistakably characterizes them."

The *mortars* were of two kinds, *stationary* and *portable.* The former were circular holes of about twelve inches in diameter, and from two to six inches in depth, cut in a smooth surface rock, situated at some convenient and accessible point. This was the neighborhood mill, driven, however, without steam or water-power. Each customer was expected to grind his own grist and take his own toll.

The portable mortars were made, some of *steatite* or soapstone, and others of *sandstone.*

The pestle and mortar process merely broke the maize in coarse fragments, and this by being boiled made the favorite Indian dish called *samp,* and from the aborigines we have adopted its use, as well as its name. But the growing fastidiousness of some Indian damsel demanding a greater variety of edibles in her culinary department, set the inventive genius of her admirer at work, and the result was the production of the *upper* and the *nether millstone.* The method of operation, like the pestle and mortar, was by *hand-power,* but the principle involved is the same as that in use in our mills at the present day. The nether millstone was a rock of smooth, even surface, and the upper, a stone suitably wrought for the purpose. This process pulverized the grain to the long-desired excellence, and *corn dodgers* flowed naturally therefrom, to the astonishment and delight of the nation. These delicious cakes were made by wrapping the moistened meal in husks of the corn, and baking them under the embers.

Our sable countrymen in "Dixie" denominate a similar article the "*hoe-cake*," which differs from the former only in the manner of cooking. The latter is baked on a *hoe* or *shovel*, held before the fire, but not as the old song says:

> "De way to bake a *hoe-cake*—Old Virginia neber tire—
> Stick de hoe-cake on de *foot*, and hold it to de fire."

The *axe* somewhat resembles our steel tool of that name. In the place of the eye for the *helve*, a groove was cut near the end, around which the *handle* was bent, and tied with rawhide.

They could have been of little use in felling timber, but besides the partial purpose of an axe in other respects, they were formidable weapons of war in close combat.

Chisels are so called from their resemblance to our steel tool of that name. In England they are called *Celts*, after the early people who used a similar article, and who formerly inhabited a great part of Central and Western Europe. The implements are now found in the *tumuli* or barrows of these early Celtic nations. They were used by our Indians for a variety of purposes, among others, for skinning animals, and also for removing the charred wood, as they burned the inner portion of the log from which they made their *canoe*, the outer surface, in the meantime, being kept wet, so as to preserve the sides and ends from burning. On these chisels were used *buckhorn handles*. The same articles, with buckhorn handles, securely fastened by an impervious cement, have been found in the bottom of the lake drained a few years ago in Switzerland.

It is very remarkable that the implements of the stone age belonging to the early people of Central Europe should be almost in all respects identical with those found in possession of the North American Indians.

Besides the ordinary sized chisel found here, usually about six inches in length, we have a huge article of the kind, weighing some fifteen pounds, with a double bevelled edge. It is supposed to have been used for cutting holes in the ice for fishing.

Another form of the chisel is quite common, resembling as nearly as possible the carpenter's gouge.

Hammers and sledges were made as described by Mr. Peale: "By *pecking* a groove around pebbles of various forms, mostly ovoid, and attaching a handle by bending around the groove a withe of wood. Over the whole was sewed filaments of tendon, '*rawhide*' in a green state, leaving only the part to be used exposed, which, after becoming dry, held all firmly together. This method of making a serviceable tool is not conjectural; such implements are still in use among tribes of Indians now existing, made exactly as described, and many of the stone heads have been found of all sizes, from a few ounces in weight to many pounds, assuming the semblance and efficiency of sledges or mauls used by modern mechanics. We are credibly informed that many of the largest size have been found in excavations of aboriginal origin, in the Lake Superior copper region, upon masses of native metal, bearing marks of their employment in the ungrateful task of detaching fragments for use or ornament."

Flint knives or cutting implements are numerous. They were made by dexterous blows with the stone hammer or sledge against the edge of a compact finely-grained rock, the fracture producing sharp-angled chips, with edges almost as keen as a knife. The usual material is *hornstone* or *jasper*, resembling what we improperly call *flint*. The knives were used for all the lighter purposes of cutting, as far as they could be applied. They were employed also in taking off the scalps of their enemies, and it is said some of the white intruders shared the same fate. They no doubt considered this

"The most unkindest *cut* of all."

"It is a curious fact, related by one of our early missionaries," says Mr. Heckewelder, "that the hair was permitted to grow only on the top of the head, thereby affording facilities for this barbarous operation. It was an act of cowardice in any one permitting his hair to grow on other portions of his head, as it would be considered as taking an undue advantage of his adversary. Another reason given was, that as a man has but one head, and as the warrior is distinguished by the number of scalps he brings in as trophies, if the Indians permitted the hair to grow all over the head as the white people do, *several* scalps might be made out of it, which would be unfair. Besides, cowards might thus without danger, share in the trophies of the brave, and dispute with him the honor of the victory."

They commenced pulling out the hair in childhood, and in a few years, it is alleged, it would cease to grow. The same practice was adopted in destroying the beard, hence the erroneous opinion that the Indians were deprived by nature of that troublesome ornament to the white man's face. A pair of mussel shells answered the purpose of *tweezers.*

The *arrow-points* are by far the most numerous of all the stone implements found in the Minisink. It is quite natural they should be. They were in more frequent use than any other, and were constantly liable to be lost; numbers may have been shot but once. The manufacture of arrow-points, then, must have occupied a large portion of the time of those skilled in the art. Places where they were made exhibit spalls and imperfect and broken specimens by the bushel.

The *bow and arrow* were the delight of the red man; they were his constant companions, his *defence*, his *support*, and his *amusement*. Killing his *enemies*, killing his *food*, and killing his *time*. The stem of the arrow was made of wood, and the "point" either inserted or tied fast to the end. Two varieties are made for this purpose, with and without the barb. The string of the bow was made of *rawhide*. They also employed the fibres of the *wild flax* for bowstrings, fish-nets, and other purposes.

Uncommon accuracy was acquired in the use of the bow and arrow; they could readily strike a point the size of a shilling piece at fifty yards distance, provided always, that the shilling covered the aforesaid point.

The *spear-heads* are from three inches to eight inches in length, fastened to a staff of convenient size and weight, the staff and point together called a spear, and were the same as those now in use in some of the countries in Europe, called *javelins*, excepting that the modern article has a steel point.

They were war weapons, and were also employed by the Indians in spearing animals and fish.

Hornstone, yellow and red *jasper*, and *chalcedony* constitute the material from which the spear-heads, as well as the arrow-points, were principally made.

The following description of the manner of making the arrow-points and spear-heads is taken from the remarks of an eye-witness among the Shastas and North California Indians, during that part of the United States Exploring Expedition involved in a journey by land, after the wreck of the "Peacock," from the Columbia River to San Francisco:*

A blow with a round-faced stone repeated upon a mass of jasper, agate, or chalcedony, until a flake was broken off of a suitable form, and which exhibited the right kind of fracture; then the edges were chipped by

* Mr. T. R. Peale, of the Scientific Corps, U. S. Exploring Expedition.

the application of a notch in a piece of horn, applied as a glazier applies the notches in the side of his diamond-handle to the edge of a pane of glass for a like purpose. The notches were of different sizes and depths, and much practice was doubtless requisite to insure success; as in the localities which furnished the material, or where it was worked (many of which spots have been examined), large quantities of flakes, and broken and unfinished spear and arrow-heads are found, proving that many of the efforts were abortive, and no exact form or certain result could emanate from even practised hands.

The forms of arrow-heads are very much varied: some were made without notches or barbs, and are usually called war-arrows; they were attached to the shaft by cement of resinous gum, which, when withdrawn, would of necessity leave the head in the wound. Others made with barbs or notches were secured by tendon lashings, in many instances put on with extreme neatness and symmetrical interlacing.

There is no limit to the variety of forms which these stone spear and arrow-heads assume. Many of them were rude and rough as the coarse hornstone of which they were made, in fact mere splintered fragments; whilst others, on the contrary, are as perfect in form as the weapon of the classic Greek, and made of the most beautiful jasper or chalcedony, almost gem-like in its beauty of color and shading.

There are instances of forms that lead to the conviction that novelty is one of the rare things of this world, as Solomon knew and told us long ago; this allusion is pointed to arrow-heads constructed with bevelled faces, so formed as to cause revolution in their flight, and thus maintain a true direction; a well-known principle employed in the modern rifle.

The varieties of the *tomahawk* are very great, and next to the arrow-point, are also the most numerous of all the articles obtained. Some of the forms are extremely rude. A half-rounded pebble of slate or sandstone was selected, corresponding in some degree to the required form, which being notched on opposite sides, a handle was fastened in the same manner as upon the axe and hammer.

On these simplest forms, no other work than the notching or cutting of the sides has been performed, and as the tomahawk appears to have been the constant companion of every Indian man and boy, these ruder varieties may have been the work of the latter. Those skilled in the art of making tools and other implements must have been exempt from the duties of war and the chase, and allowed to pursue their regular occupation, in order to enable them to arrive at the degree of perfection in the art exhibited in some of these specimens. Such skilful artisans possessed of course a reputation which they would not allow to be injured by the production of such rude forms as we find classed among the list of tomahawks.

The rougher specimens are found in almost every field near the river, whilst those so beautifully and symmetrically wrought, with holes perforated through the centre, and which are supposed to have been worn on the person, and kept in view, as badges to distinguish certain warriors, are not by any means so abundant.

The method of drilling the hard material —sandstone and jasper—of which the finer articles are made, as conceived and experimented on by Mr. Peale, is, no doubt, the true method.

It is described by him as follows:

"The ordinary holes are mere perforations, made by revolving a sharp-pointed flake of jasper, hornstone, or other hard stone, upon the object to be perforated, usually slate, limestone, or soapstone, the perforation being made from opposite sides, until the opening met at the middle; but in other and more finished works, such as those made for the insertion of handles in tomahawks and hammers, and more remarkably in smoking pipes, and the tubes which were probably used for that purpose, there is no reason to doubt that these holes were made by nearly the same means, and identically the same principles that are now used to drill glass and the hardest gems. A round stick of soft wood was revolved by rubbing the hands against it in opposite directions, with silicious sand and water continually renewed between the end of the stick and the article to be bored.

"A further supposition is not unreasonable, that a bowstring loosely drawn and passed around the stick, would give increased motion and more rapid effect to the process.

"The pages of Schoolcraft describe and illustrate similar arrangements in use among existing tribes, for producing fire by rapid friction."

In the department of *personal ornaments* are found some of the most finely executed of all the specimens of Indian craft. Not only the highest skill of the workman was required in the production of this class of articles, but his taste and judgment were also put to the test.

To produce a necklace of quartz beads, finely polished and perforated, with the meagre appliances at their command, must have required long, patient, and skilful labor. A great variety of ornaments were made of clay, shells, and the softer stones, in the similitude of flowers, birds, and insects.

If fashions then, like as at the present day, changed often, and new devices and different material were required at each whim of the fickle goddess, it must have been a severe tax upon the labor and ingenuity of the "personal ornament" makers.

The *fictile art* was extensively practised. Fragments of earthen-made articles are found in almost every field near the river, in the Minisink.

The material was prepared by pounding certain kinds of shells and mixing with suitable moistened clay; having dried this compound in the shade, it was then burned in the oven or kiln made for the purpose, and became hard, and would stand exposure to the fire.

The earthen pots are made of various sizes, holding from a pint to several gallons. The larger ones were used, among other purposes, for boiling the sap for maple sugar. Of the same material were made pitchers, vases, bowls, plates, &c.

Unbroken articles of earthenware are now rarely met with, but fragments, sometimes in large pieces, are found in quantities, some of these showing a degree of taste and skill in ornamentation. The earthen vessels supplied a *desideratum;* as the manufacture of these articles was not by any means the first of the stone age. Ruder nations cooked their food without the use of pots. This process was simple in the extreme, though quite ingenious:

"When meat was to be boiled, a hole was dug in the ground, about the size of a common pot, and a piece of the raw hide of the animal, as taken from his back, was put in the hole and pressed down with the hands close around the sides, and filled with water. At a fire which was built near by, several large stones were heated, which were successively dipped in the water until the meat was cooked."

Smoking was a habit quite prevalent among the Indians. The *pipe* or *calumet* was carved of stone or modelled in clay. Some of the latter are rude in form and structure, whilst others are artistic in design and elaborate in finish. The front of the bowl is often carved with devices representing sometimes the human face and various animals.

The *calumet* used in councils contains generally an emblem of the tribe represented. These are large and wrought with skill, and the long reed stem ornamented with gay feathers. It is used only on occasions of state, and when the deliberations are ended is handed from one to the other, commencing with those highest in authority.

It is used as a symbol or instrument of

peace or war. To accept the "calumet" is to agree to the terms of peace, and to refuse, is to reject them. The calumet of peace is used to seal or ratify contracts and alliances, to receive strangers kindly, and to travel with safety. The calumet of war, differently made, is used to proclaim war.

At the council held in Philadelphia, in 1758, Teedyuscung, the chief of the Delawares, addressed Governor Denny as follows:

"The Governor, and all you wise men present, hearken to what I am going to say: At the treaty at Easton, you desired me to hear you and publish what passed there to all the Indian nations. I promised you to do it; I gave the *Halloo*, and published it to all the Indian nations in this part of the world, even the most distant have heard me.

"The nations to whom I published what passed between us have let me, Teedyuscung, know that they heard and approved it, and as I am about so good a work, they sent this *pipe*, the same that their grandfathers used on such good occasions, and desired it might be filled with the same good tobacco, and that I, with my brother, the Governor, would *smoke* it.

"They further assured me that if at any time I should perceive any dark clouds arise, and would smoke but two or three *whiffs* out of this pipe, those clouds would immediately disappear."

The next day Governor Denny replied as follows:

"Brother: I smoked with a great deal of pleasure out of the pipe that the far Indians, formerly our good friends, sent you on this joyful occasion, and I must now desire you for them, as you represent them, to smoke out of my pipe, in which I have put some very good tobacco, such as our ancestors used to smoke together, and was at first planted here when this country was settled by *Onas* (William Penn).

"We have found by experience that whatever nations smoked out of it two or three hearty 'whiffs,' the clouds that were between us always dispersed, and so they will again, as often as they arise, if these Indians will smoke heartily of it."

Here the Governor smoked and gave it to Teedyuscung.

The *clothing* of the Indians was almost entirely made from the skins of animals, and their conical-shaped "wigwams" were also covered with the same material.

They possessed the knowledge of dressing skins in such a way as made them pliable. An Indian damsel, with the underdress of the *fawn*, and a robe in winter of the matchless fur of the *beaver*, was very comfortably, if not imposingly dressed.

Reference cannot here be made to the *customs* of these people: to do so would exceed the limits designed.

Mr. Heckewelder says:

"When the Indians were first visited by the whites, and after our people commenced to erect houses among them, they thought very strangely of the white people locking their doors, and could not for some time be made to understand the motive. When they left their homes they set up a *pestle* or *corn-pounder* against the outside of the door, which was enough to show that there was no one at home, and the premises were then considered sacred, no one thinking of entering the house. Missionaries have recorded, that as late as 1771 they have known large quantities of goods received from traders protected in no other way.'

All accounts represent the war-dances as frightful and terrible to behold. They are always performed previous to going out to an engagement, around a painted post, a sort of "recruiting station." It must have been frightful too to witness the Indian warriors return home after a successful engagement, with their prisoners and the scalps taken in battle. These last were carried in front, strung on a pole, behind which came the victorious column, rending the air with shouts. The dwelling of each warrior was ornamented with these terrible memorials of victory, together with all the accoutrements of warfare, skins of animals, &c.

"Thus all around the walls to grace,
Hung trophies of the fight or chase;
A target there, a bugle here,
A battle-axe, a hunting-spear,
And war-clubs, bows and arrows, store,
With tusked trophies of the boar.
Here grins the wolf as when he died,
And there the wild cat's brindle hide
The frontlets of the elk adorns,
Or mantles o'er the bison's horns;
Strange devices, defaced and stained,
The crimsoned streaks of blood retained,
And deer-skins, dappled, dun and white,
With otter's fur, and seals unite,
In rude and uncouth trappings all,
To garnish forth the warriors' hall."

To *jugglers, soothsayers, conjurors, astrologers,* and all the long list of impostors of that character, the poor Indians gave too much countenance. Besides the regular physicians, they had their quack doctors also, and were almost as badly afflicted in that respect as the present generation. On a small scale they had their Brandreth, Ayres, Hembold, Wishart, *ad infinitum,* and may also, perhaps, have had a type of that voluble, yet mythical personage, Mrs. Winslow.

The Lenapes were present in great numbers, Mr. Heckewelder says, at the landing of the Hollanders at Manhattan (New York), in 1620, and some traditions of the event were still preserved by their people.

They supposed the vessel at first to be a *whale,* then a great *bird* resting on the waters, and as it approached nearer supposed it to be a *house* drifting to the shore, but were terror-stricken when they saw the men descend and come in small boats to the land.

They looked upon these men as messengers sent from the Great Spirit to destroy them. They fled in numbers to the wilderness, others prostrated themselves to the earth, and filled the air with cries and lamentations.

It was a long time before the captain could cause them to become reconciled, and assure them by signs, that they were only men, like themselves, and intended them no harm.

By the bestowal of a few presents on the part of the sagacious officers, they soon won the hearts of these simple-minded people, and the god-like strangers were made welcome to the homes of the red men with joyful demonstrations.

It is not very creditable to our Holland ancestors, that this ceremony was terminated in a general scene of intoxication.

The liquor was at first partaken of with hesitation and distrust, and was utterly refused, until the officers and crew first set the vicious example.

In commemoration of this event, the Indians named the place Manahachtanieuk (Manhattan), the *island where we all got drunk.*

Indian Graves.

LAKE OF THE MOUNTAIN.

In the year 1811, John Arndt, of Easton, wrote to the Rev. Mr. Heckewelder concerning an Indian grave found at this solitary spot, near the shore of the lake. He was buried in a stone vault, "the rock having been rent apart for a considerable length, and wide enough to admit the body, and covered with large flat stones. With the skeleton were found a small brass kettle, some beads, some circular bones or ivory of the size of a silver dollar, pierced with two holes through the diameter; also a parcel of bone or ivory tubes, resembling pipe-stems, four and a half inches in length. Nearly opposite, down the mountain from this grave, on the flats or lowland, there was a large Indian burial-ground. Could this spot have been the special choice of this solitary inhabitant? Here was a lake with plenty of fish, abundance of large whortleberries, excellent hunting-grounds, &c. Can it be presumed that he was a noted chief or warrior to whom such distinguished respect was paid, as to deposit him so much nearer heaven and the Great Spirit?"

Several years ago, the author visited the Indian burial-ground at the base of the mountain alluded to in the letter of Mr. Arndt. It is situated about seven miles north of the Gap, on an elevation of two hundred or three hundred feet from the river, which it overlooks, together with a beautiful portion of the Valley of the Delaware. The ground had then just been cleared for cultivation, the forest trees had yielded to the axemen, and the virgin soil, so long held sacred by another race, was about to be violated with the plough. Three graves had already been opened, but a number of mounds were visible all over the field before the plough had done its work. The articles obtained from the three which I saw, were as follows: A large quantity of beads, variously colored, of stone and glass, and others of bone. Several clay ornaments, rounded and in shape like the beads, but larger, pierced through the centre; the image of an owl made of clay, and several round pieces of clay and bone about the size of an American half-dollar, dotted round the edge and twice through the centre. A great number of pieces of clay pipe, and fragments of other articles, so broken as to be undefined. In one of the graves some small bells were found, also fragments of blankets, the metallic remains of two guns, brass plates containing the crucifix, brass tobacco-boxes, &c. This was evidently a modern burial, as the articles must have been obtained from Europeans, as well as the glass beads mentioned above.

The place was visited by some gentlemen stopping at the Gap last summer, and permission given by the owner of the field to make excavations. One grave was found about three feet below the surface and exhumed. The skeleton was incased in a stone box. But few relics were obtained.

The following extracts from a letter written by a gentleman who, with others, visited the Indian burial-place near the Gap, in the autumn of 1865, is deemed not out of place in this connection. The letter was published in the *North American and United States Gazette:*

" A portion of the company now pleasantly sojourning here, treated themselves to-day to an excursion somewhat different from climbing Mount Minsi, Prospect Rock, the Indian Ladder, or even revelling at that crystal fount, Rebecca's Well, or that still more beautiful spot, Caldeno Falls. They visited and explored an Indian cemetery, where those who lived and loved, warred and hunted, in long anterior days, have lain in quiet, and, until recently, undisturbed repose.

"The site of this early cemetery is on the point of an elevated diluvial plain above the mouth of Brodhead's Creek. The plateau is about ninety feet above the river level, and embraces, perhaps, four acres. The view is very fine, commanding the Delaware, Shawanee Island, Cherry Valley, and the superb scenery along the outlying arms of the grand old Kittatinny. The nomadic tribes who occupied these beautiful and fertile valleys exhibited faultless taste in selecting the spot they did for the repose of their kindred.

"Of the wild tribes who once plied the light canoe on the Maccariskittang, and hunted their game along the Minisink, we have positive information of the Shawanees and Lenni Lenapes, or Delawares. The tawny warriors,—Titans of a dark and mystic race,—have left here the impress of their great and imperishable names. Mountain, valley, river, and purling brook bear the record of many a stalworth brave.

"Various localities of interest are pointed out as the sites of Indian villages and burial-grounds; but of what particular tribe or nation, not even tradition or legendary song can tell.* One of these early cemeteries has long been regarded with interest by visitors to the Gap and residents of the neighborhood. In vain, however, did those desirous of exploring it apply for permission to the proprietor of the soil. But the love of gain proved stronger than dread of superstitious awe, and a few years since certain parties met, not having the fear of Mr. Zimmerman or ghouls or goblins before their eyes, and under the cover of night and a dense young forest, perpetrated that which men of science had ineffectually attempted. The night despoilers had roughly but surely done

* The Minsi, a branch of the Lenape Indians, inhabited this portion of the Valley of the Delaware. The Shawanees were mere sojourners here.—L. W. B.

the work of exhumation in several of these interesting memorials of the dead. The parties who had despoiled the graves were actuated by a single motive,—gain. They hoped to secure valuable relics, which could be sold to curiosity-gatherers from the cities. Some of these ill-got gains were offered to gentlemen of intelligence and probity whom I have seen, who declined to purchase. Others, however, in quest of 'curiosities, did buy. It may not positively be known what articles have been taken from the despoiled graves, but I have been informed that among the articles found was a finely wrought stone pipe.

"With this digression, I will give a brief account of our operations to-day.

"We found the cemetery composed of numerous 'graves,' in close proximity to one another. These were scarcely distinguishable, so slight is the elevation. Each grave is encircled by a trench, and a group of some half a dozen had evidently been surrounded by a gravel ditch. The circumvallation was quite distinct.

"Selecting an undisturbed spot, we put a couple of stout men to work. Removing the soil, we were convinced human agency had been at work. Instead of the gravel, which marks the diluvial, we found a coarse yellow sand, intermingled with clay. At the depth of about two and a half feet, we found an ulna, or some other parts of a human frame. The skeleton was in tolerable preservation. The cranium is in good condition, with the exception of a portion of the right superior maxillary, which appeared missing. The teeth are in good preservation, but much worn by the use of maize. The sections indicate a person of about middle age. The frame was large, and doubtless that of a male. The mode of burial had been by inhumation; placing the body in a recumbent posture, extending from east to west, the face looking eastward. A slight cist had been excavated, which received the body, free from cement or stone incasement, and having placed with it the few personal articles which ornamented it in life, a careful covering of sand was made to the height of the cist, and terminating in a small tumulus. The sand had evidently been carried from the river's beach, as it is not found at a nearer point. This is a peculiarity, and worth attention. Respect for the dead would not permit him to be buried in the coarse gravel of the plain where the graves are located.

"Of the articles of personal adornment recovered were parts of two metallic ornaments, brooches, or ear-drops, found in close proximity to the head. They are an alloy, pewter perhaps, circular in form, and two inches in diameter. Also, two spiral wire sprigs of brass, one inch in length and half an inch in diameter, and three bone or shell beads, one quite large. These are by far the most valuable and interesting relics recovered, as they are purely aboriginal, while the metallic articles are of European fabrication. In addition to those discovered was the rude form of a pocket-knife, but so oxidized as to be almost undistinguishable. Of course, these articles, with the exception of the bone beads, are of white men's manufacture, and utterly valueless to the archæologist. The occupant of this humble tomb lived after interviews had been established between the whites and Indians. This discovery dispelled all illusions of great antiquity. It was interesting, however, as showing the mode of burial practised by the wild tribes who roamed these forests at the period of settlement by the whites. Such discoveries are valuable to science, and the gentlemen who made the researches considered themselves amply remunerated for their trouble.

"The cranium is worthy the attention of ethnologists. It is properly orthognathous, resembling the round-headed Calmuck, figured by Huxley. The forehead is tolerably full, the zygomatic processes prominent, but not the maxillary and orbital conformations which distinguish the common Indian. These indicia, with a fair facial angle, might raise a doubt with some as to the true character of the person buried, were it not for counterbalancing proofs. Part of the right superior maxillary being gone, it is somewhat difficult to determine how much of a prognathous form there may be, which is an almost unfailing characteristic of all nomadic races. I write these hasty notes without having given the skull a careful examination. Perhaps further examination may support some additional facts. It is in possession of my friend, L. W. Brodhead, Esq., and will constitute a feature in his collection of antiquities for this locality. To Mr. B. the public are mainly indebted for these explorations."

LEGENDS.

Winona; or, The Story of Lover's Leap.

AN HISTORICAL LEGEND.

"She loves,—but knows not whom she loves,
  Nor what his race, nor whence he came;
Like one who meets, in Indian groves,
  Some beauteous bird without a name,
Brought by the last ambrosial breeze,
From isles in th' undiscover'd seas,
To show his plumage for a day
To wondering eyes, and wings away."

MOORE.

Two centuries ago there reigned, in the valley of the Minisink, a noble chieftain named Wissinoming. He was the head of that once most powerful and ancient people, known as the "Lenni Lenape." Their possessions extended from the highest sources of the rivers Delaware and Susquehanna to the ocean, and every valley and hill-top drained by their tributaries echoed the praises of Lenape's chieftain.*

The Lower Minisink was the headquarters of this nation. Here Wissinoming resided, and here emanated the decrees dispatched by fleet-footed couriers, in case of war or apprehended danger, or signalled by "fire-lights" kindled on a hundred hill-tops,† which reassured, and thus preserved the unity of the confederate tribes. For how many centuries Wissinoming's ancestors reigned in this beautiful valley, and plied their boats on these quiet waters, and chased the deer in these forests, and defied their enemies in these rocky fastnesses, and worshipped on these mountain-heights, time will never reveal to us. And when the red

* "The compound word *Lenni Lenape* signifies '*original people*,' a race of beings who are the same that they were from the beginning, acknowledged by near forty Indian tribes as being their grandfathers. All these tribes, derived from the same stock, recognize each other as *Wapanachki* or *Lenape*, which among them is a generic name."—*Heckewelder*.

† It is a well-established fact that "signal lights" were used by the Indians, and that important intelligence was communicated from one eminence to another, hundreds of miles away, with the certainty, and almost the celerity, of electricity. The adoption of a similar system proved of great importance to our army in the late Rebellion.

man first visited the shores of our continent, whether before or after the departure of the Israelites from Egypt, is not material to our present story.

Winona was the beloved and only daughter of Wissinoming. She and her brother Manatamany were the pride of this noble chieftain, and were the objects of his greatest care and solicitude; all the instruction that a wise but uncultivated parent could impart were bestowed on these children. They, consequently, grew up at least free from the ruder habits of their people, and Winona manifested a character of great strength and beauty. Her father had impressed her with the fact, that she was of the descent of a noble race of chieftains, and that her people could claim great antiquity, and she readily saw that they were greatly superior to all the other tribes whose representatives at times visited her father's home.

The Lenape were bold and fearless, but considerate and just; and having enjoyed years of peace, paid some attention to the cultivation of the soil, and were acquiring habits bordering on civilization; and when the whites first appeared among them, that civilization was ready to dawn. The first settlers were, therefore, received with open arms. They continued their friendly intercourse, and were not averse to their permanent residence amongst them. The improved methods to promote comfortable existence by the new-comers, their ready discernment led them to at least appreciate, if not to adopt, and all that was now needed was fair and honorable dealing; and had the policy of the elder Penn been continued, it is fair to presume that the Lenape would have at this day existed in this valley, a comparatively enlightened and cultivated people.

The first appearance of the whites was only to explore the country. They were from the Holland settlement on the Hudson. They found a considerable extent of land under cultivation, and were delighted with its appearance, and with the friendship manifested by the natives, and soon thereafter arrangements were made for the introduction of a colony. A number of families at length arrived, and formed the first settlement in the Minisink country, and perhaps in the State.

Winona seemed to be drawn instinctively to the society of the cultivated ladies forming the settlement. On account of her position as the daughter of an illustrious chief, she was well received. Her beauty of person, her dignified but gentle manners, her desire to learn of the white ladies and adopt their customs, soon made her a great favorite, and she came to be styled by them, *Princess* Winona. She continued to be ever after the firm friend of the whites, and proved herself, on more than one occasion, a very Pocahontas, indeed.

The exploring party, just named, with the prevailing thirst for gold, had discovered in the mountain at Pahaqualong, a few miles above, evidences of what they supposed to be a rich mine of copper, and the information having been forwarded to their mother country, a company was speedily formed under the auspices of the Holland Government, and an expedition fitted out and placed in charge of a young man of rank named Hendrick Van Allen.* He was a gentle-

* These mines were worked to a considerable extent, but with what success is not known. They are situated near the base of the Kittatinny Mountain, eight miles above the Del-

man of fine accomplishments, pleasing address, and fair exterior, full of adventure, and the kind of wild frontier life he was for a time obliged to lead, seemed well suited to his inclinations. He soon became accustomed to the hardships incident to a life where few evidences of civilization were to be witnessed, much less enjoyed.

He visited the settlement a few miles below, soon after his arrival, and there heard, at the house of one of the colonists, the fame of the "Indian Princess." The thought of *Prince* or *Princess* had not entered Hendrick's mind since he left the land of civilization, and he supposed himself now far beyond the influences of nobility; hence to hear of an embryo "Queen" in this remote wilderness struck him as rather ludicrous. He, however, promised his friend to see her when he visited the settlement again.

aware Water Gap, on the New Jersey side of the river. A company was organized, about twenty years ago, in New York, for the purpose of re-working them, but failed of success. When they commenced operations, they found large trees growing upon places where excavations had been made nearly two hundred years before. The place is now called *Pahaquarri*, a corruption of "Pahaqualong," the original name.

The young adventurer having satisfied his own mind that about one-half of the Kittatinny Mountain was composed of copper ore, he commenced the construction of the Great Wagon Road from Pahaqualong to the Hudson River, a distance of one hundred miles. Whilst this work was in progress, he employed himself in the sports of the chase. He fancied himself an expert in the use of the rifle, and found the wild game as abundant as he could wish.

At Hendrick's next visit to the settlement, he met the young "Princess" at the house of his friend, where, ever since their arrival, she had been a frequent and welcome visitor. Hendrick expected to see in the daughter of the famous chief less rudeness of manner, perhaps, than in the other daughters of the forest; but he was unprepared for what he now witnessed.

Winona's modesty, refinement, and dignified deportment were unaccountable to him; and though he had heard her beauty highly praised, she far excelled in his mind the most favorable descriptions given of her. Not having measured the character of her mind, he introduced such conversation as he thought adapted to her understanding and suited to her inclinations. He spoke of the enjoyment he had experienced in imitating the free and unrestrained life of her people; the excitement of the chase; the unbounded park filled with game that had not yet learned to flee at the report of his gun, and was not too modest to mention the skill he had acquired in its use by frequent practice. Winona, though accustomed to the wild sports of her people, and confident of her skill in the use of the bow and arrow, having often employed them as an exercise and an amusement, was more modest in the estimate of her prowess; and Hendrick learned, too, from the tenor of her conversation, that there were other themes better suited to the character of Winona's mind, and more pleasing for her contemplation. A friendship, very natural under the circumstances, was at once formed, and Hendrick henceforward fancied that the better hunting-grounds were in the direction of the new settlement and Winona's home.

Not long after this event the old chief Wissinoming died. It was the saddest period of Winona's life. She grieved, not only on account of her own loss, but she mourned also the loss her nation had sustained. The affairs of her people were in a critical condition. The Lenape had been invaded by some tribes from the North, and though the latter had been severely chastised during her father's reign, Winona and her brother, Manatamany, feared a renewal of hostilities.

The following incidents, though having no direct connection in this narrative, are still important, as relating to the Lenape nation, and on that account their recital will, perhaps, be justified.

The power of the Lenape was undisputed, and they had enjoyed untold years of undisturbed quiet; but before the reign of Wissinoming, a cloud had gathered in the North. Some ambitious tribes had commenced invading their territory, and though they had always been repulsed with severe losses, the Lenape were at length confronted by that powerful union of hostile tribes, composed of the Mohawks, Onondagas, Senecas, Oneidas, Cayugas, and Tuscaroras, and known as the "Six Nations." The clouds that had been gathering culminated, and a terrific storm burst upon the devoted heads of the Lenape. The war raged for many years, with varying success; the people of the Minisink maintained their ancient prestige, though other portions of the Lenape nation were forced to succumb, or accept annihilation. It was not until near the middle of the eighteenth century, when the Six Nations received the countenance and encouragement of the whites, that the Minsi,—the elder sons and occupants of the ancient heritage of the Lenape,—yielded to power and intrigue. The conduct of certain of the whites at the memorable conventions held at Philadelphia and Easton,—where the Delawares (as they were now called) were browbeaten and disgraced, and their chief, on one occasion, led out of the convention by the hair of his head by an upstart of the Six Nations,—is unaccountable upon any other hypothesis, than that by the dispersion of the Delawares, and by the encouragement extended to the Six Nations, they could more readily gain possession of territory to which neither themselves nor the Six Nations had a shadow of claim.

It has been alleged that the Delaware

chief behaved cowardly on this occasion. The assertion is unwarranted by the facts. Surrounded by enemies greatly superior in numbers to his own people, and who were supported by the wealth and influence of the English, he well knew that resistance would end in the destruction of his remaining followers. Hence, the course he pursued is such as a wise man would have adopted.

At a subsequent council, held at Easton, it is said, "the English had made so many presents to the Six Nations, that they would hear no explanations from the Delawares." Well might Tedyuskung have said, with reference to the whites, "*And you, too, my brothers!*"

To the credit of William Penn and his *true* followers, be it ever remembered, that they did not desert the Delawares in their extremity, but stood up for them on all occasions, and condemned the unjust treatment they received.

The subjugation of this people, and their exile from the Valley of the Delaware, form one of the saddest episodes in the history of nations. Is it to be wondered that they lingered long upon the waters of their favorite river? That they viewed with terror, from the heights of the Kittatinny, the approach of the white man to take possession of the homes they were compelled by their enemies to abandon? To be despoiled of all they held dear, even the places made sacred by the dead of centuries? I fancy I can see them as they meet in the last hurried council: no fire is kindled; no glad voices are heard; no songs of mirth and rejoicing, naught but a saddening wail, the requiem of departing glory. The corn and dried venison are collected together. The aged chief, who has cheered his followers in the thick strife of contending hosts, now trembles with emotion at his exile from the land he loves. Hear him, for his utterance is choked: "Let us take a last lingering look as the departing rays of light are shed upon the Blue Hills, and then go hence to that strange land, whilst the sun sleeps behind the mountain, that the white robber may not laugh at our tears."

This digression has led to a view of the condition of the Lenapes, nearly a century subsequent to the main incidents of our story. At the death of Wissinoming, Manatamany was looked upon as the natural and legitimate successor to his father, whom he much resembled in strength of mind and heroic deportment. Being younger, however, than his sister Winona, she was looked up to as the "guardian angel" of her people; and as much consulted in matters of state as her brother. To add to their other troubles, a serious outbreak now occurred between a portion of their people and the colonists, in which a young man, a favorite of the colonists, was killed. Much excitement was manifested by both parties. The cause of the quarrel was the attempted occupancy and cultivation, on the part of the settlers, of the *Great Shawano Island* opposite the Indian town of Wyomissing. This island was a favorite resort of the Indians, and was a cherished part of their possessions. Its great productiveness* excited the cupidity

* That these islands in the Delaware, as well as the adjacent main land, were under cultivation by the Indians, there is scarcely a doubt remaining. The evidence of the early settlers on the subject is confirmed by the discovery, a few years ago, on Shawnee Island, of a dozen or more articles of the *stone age*, differing from those ordinarily found, which, on being submitted to Mr. Franklin Peale, of Philadelphia,—

of the colonists, and frequent attempts had been made for its purchase; but no offer, however liberal, would be entertained for a moment. In the quarrel Manatamany took no part, though his heart was with his people. Winona, the friend of the colonists, as well as the beloved oracle of her own nation, was looked to by the friends of peace in both parties, as the only hope of an amicable settlement of the difficulty. Winona felt the responsibility of her position, but did not shrink from the performance of her duty.

The town of Wyomissing was the ancient home of the Lenape chieftains. In front of the lodge of Winona and her brother, were assembled the excited multitude. On the rocky parapet, bordering her little flower-garden, stood the Queen of the Forest, the heroine and orator of the occasion; to her, all eyes were directed; to her, all were ready to listen with reverence, and now waited in breathless silence the Sibylline utterances:

"Winona is the daughter of Wissinom-

perhaps the best authority on this subject in the country,—were unhesitatingly pronounced implements of agriculture, answering the purpose of our common hoe.

ing, who lies sleeping on yonder hill-top, overlooking the waters of Lenape's river. The island, the cause of this quarrel, also lies before him. For how many centuries Wissinoming's fathers reigned in the Minisink, Winona knoweth not; but the moons will count in number as the hairs of Winona's head. Winona's father sometimes speaks from the spirit-land, and Winona hears his words of love and wisdom in the whispering winds. She listens to catch the music of his voice to-day; but the winds do not speak, and Winona's heart is heavy with grief. Winona loves the people of her fathers, and desires to do them good. She rejoices in their successes, and mourns over their misfortunes. Their song of joy, or wail of grief, is echoed in Winona's heart. Winona's heart is sad now! Winona loves her white neighbors also, and hoped to live with them in peace and friendship forever. Their ladies are kind and gentle to Winona, and have taught her many ways that Winona loves, and filled her mind with many wonderful thoughts that are beautiful, and that Winona dreamed not of. Winona's heart is very sad! The weight of grief would melt in tears, but Winona cannot weep now. Winona loves not strife nor bloodshed; but Winona is not herself afraid to die.

"A young man has been slain by our people. He was much beloved by our neighbors. Who committed the fatal deed we know not. It is but justice, and according to the custom of our own nation, that his death should be avenged, and one of our number be offered to appease the just wrath of our neighbors. Winona is not afraid to die! Hear, then, what Winona saith: On the morrow, on the first wake of the morning, before the sun shows his face from behind the hills of the Kittatinny, lét Winona be slain by the hands of her own people, and let her be buried beside her noble father, Wissinoming. Let Hendrick be called from the mountain; let him raise Winona's head, as in the custom of the burial of my people,* that the earth may rest lightly upon it, and let him pray to *his* God for the spirit of Winona. The Shawano Island is loved by our people. It is fair to look upon, and the

* It was the custom of the Indians to bury distinguished persons of their own tribe with the head elevated to nearly a sitting posture, and to encase the body in a stone box.

corn has ripened upon it for my people for more summers than the numbers of our nation. Winona's canoe has passed many times around it, and touched at every shore.

"The white man must not take it from my people; but let my good brother give to them the Island *Manwallamink*, and may the dove of peace descend, and hover over the people of my fathers and our white neighbors forever!"

A saddening wail, mingled with murmurs of discontent, rose upon the still air, and Manatamany essayed to give utterance to these incoherent mutterings; but the shouts of the colonists drowned his voice: "*Winona must not, shall not die!* She shall live to bless us and you! We ask no sacrifice; we only ask, that if it please Manatamany, Winona may be adopted as our sister, and be to us, as to you, a princess and 'guardian angel.'"

This interesting event proved most auspicious; years of uninterrupted friendship followed, and, indeed, its influence was never entirely lost upon either the natives or the colonists. The settlement increased in numbers, and amity reigned, and an apparent desire to benefit the condition of each by the other manifested itself upon all occasions. How easily this policy might have been continued, and how glorious would have been its results! All that was now needed was honesty of purpose, and a little forbearance. How readily on all occasions might the truths of the Christian religion be introduced among a people who are strangers to its teachings, if its beautiful precepts were practised by those desiring its promulgation! Winona had become to the colony an object of love and veneration, and continued to be the idol of her people; and when Hendrick visited the settlement again, he found the praises of Winona on every tongue. His visits now became more frequent, and he found himself fascinated by Winona; and yet it does not appear that he took much thought beyond the present pleasure of her society; into the future he did not stop to gaze. He had now become more occupied in his duties at the mines; the hours of relaxation, however, afforded him, were entirely devoted to her, not dreaming that he was awakening a passion of dangerous intensity in the susceptible heart of

Winona. She at first seemed to look upon Hendrick in the character of a brother and instructor in things that delighted her and filled her mind with wonder; and such he had been to her. He had taught her many customs and things that were entirely new, and she was a most apt pupil.

Riding on horseback, though practised by the male members of her people, could not be indulged in to any extent by Winona, as the condition of the roads (being mere trails or footpaths) forbade it. But Hendrick now used his new road, originally constructed for the transportation of ores from the mines, to a more satisfactory purpose, and much to the delight of this flower of the forest. In the absence of Hendrick, it was the custom of Winona to spend much of her time alone, and with her little red canoe, and bow and arrow, she passed many hours in that portion of the river which flows between the islands and the mainland on which Wyomissing was situated. The borders of this stream were skirted on both sides, then as now, by a growth of large and beautiful trees, some of which are still standing, no doubt, upon which Winona once gazed with delighted admiration, and from whose uppermost branches the wild-fowl and other game, then so abundant, were brought down with absolute certainty, when she was inclined to exercise her skill with the bow and arrow. On one of these occasions, when Winona's canoe was gliding leisurely over these quiet waters, she heard on the island, and quite near her, the report of a rifle. At first, the report of a gun was a terror to Winona; but Hendrick's visits to the settlement being now always announced in that way, it had become, instead, a feeling of delight, and her first thoughts now were of the near presence of Hendrick. She moored her boat to the shore, and quietly waited and watched. Hendrick continued to fire, and she soon discovered a black squirrel upon one of the loftiest branches of a large tree near her. Taking up her bow, and selecting from her quiver a choice arrow, with deliberate, well-directed aim, she brought down the animal bleeding at Hendrick's feet. He picked up the squirrel, thinking it had fallen from the effect of the discharge of his own gun a moment before, but was greatly astonished to find it pierced with an arrow still sticking in its body. Recollecting to have seen Winona's skill with the bow and arrow before, he at once divined her near presence, and soon sought out his fair rival, with her little bark moored under the edge of the beach, near where he stood. This unexpected meeting gave mutual delight. Hendrick complimented Winona on her prowess, and though she could not indulge him with equal compliment, she gave expression only to the pleasure the circumstance of their meeting afforded her; and before parting, on this occasion, Hendrick should have discovered the spark he was kindling, and the danger of fanning to a flame that which, in a breast like Winona's, would continue to burn forever.

It would be most interesting to know the manner and character of thought indulged in by a child of nature with the active powers of mind possessed by Winona, before coming in contact with any other light than that furnished by the vague traditions of her own people. Winona spent many hours with no other companion than her little boat; these were her hours of solitude.

That great mind could not be idle. Of what did she muse? She could not wander in thought far back into the past, and if so, the traditions of her people were not sufficient to supply much food for thought, and the successive days of the passing present were a uniform round of uninteresting sameness. She could, perhaps, run over in her mind the uncertain stories of a long line of noble chieftains, and could recite deeds of daring heroism performed; but Winona needed something more than all this. Her mind yearned for more refined food for thought. Yearned for the light, that light her penetrating vision had caught in faint glimmerings through the misty clouds that had inveiled her people for centuries. Could she behold the sun as it rose from behind the great mountain, and picture to herself that it had for some hours before it appeared to her, lighted up cities filled with gay and lively people,—such as she since came in contact with, and which had given her so much pleasure,—without any other light than that furnished by her own unassisted imagination? She may have heard her noble father speak of the "great flood of waters," lying towards both the rising and setting sun, and may have accompanied him on one of his visits of state to where the blue waters of the great ocean were revealed to her astonished vision. If so, could it have been to her mind only an unending flood, extending beyond the utmost stretch of her imagination into vast illimitable infinity? or could she, by the powers of her mind, give to its bounds comprehension, and to its measure limits?

Might she not in these hours of solitude have been led to inquire into the first great cause, and by communion in spirit with her Heavenly Father have had revealed to her by impressions we, who have clearer light, do not conceive of, the blessed story of Redemption? It would be terrible to think, that that communion could not be enjoyed by the multitudes who, like Winona, must have felt an "aching void" without it, and who may have lived lives of comparative freedom from actual transgression.

It is natural to suppose that after Winona's introduction into the society of the colonists her mind took a different turn, and that she now had new elements of thought furnished her; and during her interviews with Hendrick at this period, which had become quite frequent, the whole effort of her mind was employed in making him the active medium of intelligent thought. She labored for new ideas, new facts, and new emotions. She was inquisitive without the power of asking directly for that which gave her so much delight to hear; and her efforts, therefore, were incessant to make Hendrick talk, and he could converse on no subject without affording her both instruction and pleasure. To Hendrick this was the most agreeable and interesting of employments, and such promptings as he received were calculated to bring into active employment the full measure of his capacity. Winona was a charming listener, and he an equally good talker,—the former quality almost as rare in the general world as the latter. Hendrick was intelligent and observing, and had seen much of that world he was revealing to her, which Winona termed "the world of light," and all his recitals were to her astonishing.

After the conclusion of one of his lively descriptions, Winona appeared sad, and he was at no loss to divine the cause. She grieved that she could give but such poor return for the great boon to her of Hendrick's conversation; and felt so much her inferiority in this respect as to cause her on this, and other occasions, to shrink away in sadness and dejection. But Hendrick saw in her a precious bud awaiting the light and heat of the sun of intelligence to develop the beautiful, fragrant, full-blown rose of lovely womanhood. She would try, however, to interest him in subjects relating to her own people. She spoke of the wealth of her nation in unbounded forests, plains, and rivers; the numerous tribes whose chiefs looked up to her people and called them "Fathers;" the heroism and endurance of the warriors of her nation; scenes of the chase in which she was permitted to participate; some remarkable skill displayed in the use of the bow and arrow. But she felt, at the same time, the meagreness of the intellectual repast she was furnishing to him whom it would be her highest ambition and enjoyment to please. On one subject, however, she did not hesitate to speak with some degree of confidence, and with the assurance that its contemplation would be a source of delight to Hendrick, as it always was to herself: *the great natural beauty of the country she inhabited.*

She spoke in raptures of the grand old river that lay before them; of the lovely Valley of the Minisink, of many days' travel in extent, which the waters of this river adorned. She described the numerous waterfalls on its tributaries, and gave the euphonious and expressive titles by which they were known. And, above all, the majesty of the surrounding hills, and that grand stretch of mountain bordering the river that shut out the light of early day, and which had no ending.*

She spoke of the old tradition of this beautiful valley having once been a deep sea of water, and the bursting asunder of the mountains at the will of the Great Spirit, to uncover for the home of her people the vale of the Minisink; the mighty chasm in the mountain, and the twin giants overlooking the vast extent of country to the rising sun, as far as the eye can reach. Hendrick had

* *Kitochtanemin*, Kittatinny, endless mountain.

only seen the *Delaware Water Gap** from the town where Winona resided. She now proposed to him a visit from Wyomissing in her canoe to the foot of the cliff, and to ascend by the Indian trail to the summit, and Hendrick's next visit was agreed upon for this excursion.

In the meantime, the English government had obtained possession of New York, and after the surrender of Stuyvesant, the Dutch Governor, orders were sent out to Van Allen to abandon the mining operations in the Minisink, and to report to his government without delay.† The news fell like a leaden weight upon Hendrick's heart; all his fair prospects were blasted in a moment, and his first thoughts were, how to break the sad intelligence to Winona.

* The "Gap" was called by the Indians *Pohoqualin*, which word signifies the termination of two mountains with a stream passing between them.

The river was called Lenapewihittuck, the river of the Lenape. Mack-er-isk-iskan, seems to have been a *place* in the river, and not the name of the river itself.

† In the expedition fitted out by the English government, in 1664, which captured New Netherlands (New York) from the Dutch, the writer's great-great-great-grandfather was a captain.

He met her at the appointed time. She appeared lovelier than ever before, and manifested more than her accustomed vivacity. She was dressed mostly after the custom of her white lady friends, through whom she had ordered from abroad, a habit of rich crimson cloth, trimmed with gold lace, made somewhat after the style, which in modern days has vainly struggled for supremacy, known as the "Bloomer." She wore her long hair in plaits reaching near her feet. Her head was usually adorned with a wreath made from the gay plumage of birds; but was now crowned with wild flowers. Her jewels were the finer quality of the minerals common to the country. She wore a necklace of beads composed of crystallized quartz, party-colored jasper, and some of the varieties of agate.* And estimating their value by the amount of labor bestowed upon their finish, they would rival the more costly of those worn by modern belles.

Winona made the best use of her knowl-

* Some stone beads, of the above-described material, have been obtained from Indian graves along the river, of such finished workmanship, as almost to baffle modern skill, assisted by modern appliances.

edge of the locality, and conducting the canoe herself, she let it glide so quietly over the waters as to afford the best opportunity for witnessing the different objects of interest, none of which escaped Winona's observation. And she gave such vivid descriptions of the lovely scenes before them as to startle Hendrick from the sad reverie in which he was indulging. At the junction of the Analoming with the Delaware, which she termed "the marriage of the waters," she rested her boat to point out one of the favorite haunts of her youth, in the grove bordering these two streams, and where her father first permitted her to prove her skill with the bow and arrow, on as large and highly prized game as the forest elk; and though he stood with his own bow ready drawn, he did not have occasion to speed the arrow, as hers proved quite effectual.

The contrast between this and former meetings of Winona and Hendrick was marked. Winona now afforded the intellectual entertainment. They each had acquired a good knowledge of the other's language; but, at the request of Hendrick, on this occasion Winona spoke in her native tongue, and he thought her truly eloquent. In their ascent up the mountain, Winona proved herself familiar with every crag and cliff; every murmuring rill or gurgling brook, to most of which she had herself been the intelligent nomenclatress; and she discovered and pointed out beauty everywhere, from the mossy carpet under their feet to the extended panorama from the towering summit; and but for the sorrowful revelation Hendrick was soon to make, this would have been the charmed day of their lives. They had now descended from Mount Minsi, and were seated on a mossy bed overlooking the river as it slowly wound its way through the narrowing gorge. Hendrick had tried to conceal the burden that was pressing so heavily upon him; but Winona had discovered his unwonted quiet, and after having several times rallied him from his abstracted moods, she now, in sympathy with him, was silent and contemplative.

This silence reigned for several minutes; the fated moment had now arrived. Hendrick could not endure the thought of leaving without communicating the cause of his separation; and though he loved Winona sufficiently well to make her his bride, his relation to his government was such as to forbid the possibility of his taking her with him as his wife, even if she should consent to such an arrangement (her relation to, and fondness for her own people rendering it quite improbable), and Hendrick did not dare to hold out the promise of ever being able to return to claim her in her own country, though he entertained a secret hope that such happiness might be in store. It does not appear, however, that Hendrick dreamed of the extent of Winona's passion for him, and how it had deepened since their last meeting.

At length, he drew forth the fatal letter containing the peremptory orders from his government, and made known to Winona its startling contents.

She gave vent to no unusual emotions; did not shriek; did not shed a tear; did not even murmur at the terrible blow that fell upon her with a force sufficient to crush a weaker mind to earth. She paused but for a moment, then standing firm and erect as the forest oak, displaying the heroism of her noble ancestry, but, alas, resolved upon a purpose so common with her people, and which Hendrick did not in time discover.

With unfaltering voice she addressed him in the following words:

"Winona's sun has set forever!
She awakes from a beautiful dream;
But such a dream,
The gladdening beams of morning light
Do not dispel.
O thou loveliest of Winona's images!
Thou fairest of her creations,
And thou skilfullest of limners!
Canst thou behold the picture
Thy noble self hath painted,
On the virgin heart of Winona?
It shall not be blotted out;
Winona will wear it
In the spirit land,
And cherish it there.
Winona doubteth not
The love that Hendrick bears her;
But the fashion of his love
Is not like Winona's.
Hendrick's love may melt away
Like the snows of winter
In a new sunlight.
The current of the deep river
Flows on forever;
So does the love of Lenape's daughter.
But Winona will not stay
To stem the current alone.
The Great Spirit who rules the heavens
Is the father of Winona's people:
He calls Winona home.

Hendrick's duty bids him away
Beyond the great waters.
Let him go hence,
Beloved of Winona!
Winona would not chide
The dear author of these fleeting joys;
The unwilling cause
Of this deadliest sorrow.
Winona would die,
And live to die again,
Once more to feel the gentle current,
The rising, swelling, joyous torrent,
Flowing from this fount of love.
Farewell, brother!
Tutor, lover!
Winona's sun has set forever."

In a moment she disappeared from view. Hendrick ran to the cliff, caught her in his arms; they reeled on the precipice, and—

A Legend of the Delaware Water Gap.

BY MRS. E. S. SWIFT.

> "And then their love was secret. O, it is
> Most exquisite to have a fount of bliss
> Sacred to us alone!"
>
> MISS LANDON.

I WAS spending a week with a party of friends, at the Delaware Water Gap. We had just returned from a delightful ramble through the woods to Flat Rock, and were seated on the piazza of the hotel, watching the lights and shadows of the passing clouds on the Jersey Mountain, which rose to the height of sixteen hundred feet, immediately opposite to us. The day, though late in August, was as capricious as one in April. Sunshine and showers had alternated with the hours; the sun, a few moments previous, had been bathing the wooded summit of the mountain in a flood of golden radiance, piercing the thickets of underwood, and revealing to the curious eye many a leafy nook of vernal beauty; now it was raining heavily, and the·dull plashing sound of the rain-drops, as they fell upon the river immediately beneath us, imparted to us all a sensation of melancholy. We were suddenly aroused by Emilie exclaiming: "Look down the Gap; see, the sun is already shining there; surely this place is bewitched; do look at the rainbow on the water!"*

We all arose, and gazed in the direction to which she pointed our attention, and one of the most vivid-colored rainbows I ever beheld, lay pictured across the river from shore to shore. In vain we strained our eyes in all directions towards the sky; the dull, leaden-hued clouds above us gave no history of the beautiful vision. For a few minutes the bow of promise rested on the stormy waters, then its rich painting of many colors faded from our sight.

In about half an hour the sun was again shining merrily, and every leaf and sprig seemed hung with precious gems. The air was laden with the perfume from the woods, and as the cool breezes swept across the piazza, we knew they had passed over lone coverts of romantic beauty, where fairies

* The landlord of the Gap Hotel told us that, once before, he had witnessed a similar sight.

might hide, and where the ferns, the mosses, and the wild-flowers grew. We had worn out dresses and shoes in our daily visits to the Pennsylvania and Jersey Mountains; we had been pioneered by our good-natured landlord and his pretty little twins to all the known lions of the Gap; but we were hourly making voyages of discovery for ourselves; and when we assembled around the well-provided table of our host, each had his or her adventure to relate. One had found out an echo in the deep forest that answered to every word; another had been botanizing, and the mantel-stand was filled with tumblers of gorgeous-colored flowers; another, a disciple of old Isaac Walton, had been angling, and a dish of fine sunfish attested his success. In the evenings, the piazza was our favorite promenade. We had some delightful musicians with us, and in music and conversation the hours glided away with such rapidity, that we always expressed surprise at the shortness of the evening, when our host announced that eleven o'clock had struck. Our party consisted of six ladies and four gentlemen, all unmarried; but, very unfortunately, we were too closely related for Cupid to show his face amongst us.

"What!" I hear my reader exclaim, "no love! I would not give a fig for such a story." Nor I either, dear reader; particularly as the scene is laid in the Delaware Gap—the very headquarters of the wily god, where nature, in her most glorious dress, keeps jubilee;

"And where, beneath, around, above,
Earth, water, air, seem full of love."

Ah! the deep recesses of those forest shades, the close intricacies of those verdant aisles, how often have their silence and solitudes been the chosen sanctuaries for love's impassioned confessions; and hearts have been united in those solemn old woods, never again to be riven asunder; and there, perchance,

"Young hearts were plighted when the storms
Were dark upon life's sky,
In full, deep knowledge of their task,
To suffer and to die."

"The rain was over and gone," and the afternoon was so serene and beautiful, we all sailed down to the shore, and soon filled the only boat belonging to the establishment. Josephine, a very lovely girl from Baltimore, sat, like the queen of beauty, on the prow of the boat, singing snatches of old songs, in the gayety of her heart. She was one of the brightest-looking beings I ever beheld; tall and graceful, with a face of uncommon loveliness; her complexion was soft and transparent, and the slightest emotion tinted her delicate cheek with the glow of damask rose; her eyes of dark blue were shaded by long black lashes, which imparted a peculiar tenderness to their expression; her hair, also black, clustered in short thick curls around her small and finely shaped head. Occasionally, she would pause in her songs, and a shade of sorrow, it might be of memory, would flit across her face. An enthusiast in her love of nature, she sat gazing upon the beautiful scenery, now warbling like a bird, and anon calling our attention to some bold projecting cliff, that looked from its elevation ready to fall and crush us.

As our boat glided into the deep waters of the Gap, we all kept silence. Shut out from the world by the towering mountains on each side of us, with naught but the sky above, and the dark river rolling beneath us, an awe as of some mighty presence fell upon our spirits; and as we emerged from the solemn gloom of that magnificent scene, the tones of our voices were more softened, conversation took a more serious cast, and we felt like those who had recently been engaged in some holy religious service.

But, full of life and youth, as a few rapid strokes of the oar brought our boat into the glad sunshine, we again awakened the echoes with songs and laughter. Cousin Tom, as we called a fine-looking young man of five-and-twenty, had arrayed himself in all the various-colored shawls of the party, and from his picturesque appearance, might have been mistaken for Osceola, or some other renowned Indian warrior; he now proposed to land us on the Jersey shore, just at the point where the river makes an abrupt turn, one of the most romantic spots imaginable. Here, while we were seated on the trunk of an enormous tree, that had been struck by lightning some years previous, and still laid as it had fallen, close to the shore, Emilie impatiently exclaimed—

"What a pity it is that there is no legend connected with this sublime place; how delightful it would be now to listen to some interesting story of the past."

"Why, ladies!" replied her brother, "among so many fair creatures, surely you have some modern reminiscences that would make very pretty wayside tales; some diary of a heart, for instance; some stray leaves from Love's Album."

"Yes," said Cousin Tom, "I am sure these girls have lots of love secrets; here is Josa, now, looking so demure and modest, she has never arrived at the age of twenty without making some acquaintance with Cupid, I know; come, blossom, let us have the last passion."

We all turned our eyes on Josephine; but the agitation and annoyance depicted on her sweet face was distressing; her brow and cheek for a moment mantled with the tell-tale crimson, and, the next instant, the pallor of death settled on every feature. Cousin Tom, in his careless badinage, had evidently touched a wound, not yet closed. An embarrassing silence followed; but we were relieved by Emilie exclaiming—

"See, we shall have company, at last, at the Gap House; there are two gentlemen on horseback on the opposite side."

For a short period they were seen slowly ascending the rough and hilly road; but the thick hedge of laurels by which it was bordered, soon concealed them from our view. Our next movement was to try and arrive at the Hotel before them, and make ourselves presentable at supper, for the sun had already disappeared, and the twilight, which in this mountainous pass is so rapidly succeeded by night, was fast approaching. Hitherto, we had been the only visitors at the Gap, and had the house all to ourselves; consequently, being a family party, we were not as particular in our costumes as we would have been had strangers been present. A half an hour of fast rowing soon brought us to the landing-place at the foot of the rocks, close to the Hotel; and we had just time to arrange our dresses and meet together on our favorite lounge, the piazza, when the sound of hoofs warned us that the travellers had arrived; but, strange to say, but one solitary horseman appeared. Here, then, was a mystery. What had become of the other? We had all distinctly seen two gentlemen, and there was no other house on the road, except an old dilapidated tavern, far down in the gloomiest part of the Gap, a place we were sure no traveller in his senses would halt at, with our commodious Hotel in prospect, for, as it was situated upon a high hill, it could be seen from a considerable distance.

Cousin Tom capered about as if he had gone mad, declaring "it was delightful, a perfect Radcliffe adventure; he had no doubt the next morning the traveller would be found concealed in a laurel thicket, stark dead, with a bowie-knife sticking in his heart."

Emilie laughed, and averred "that hereafter she should be a convert to old Cotton Mather; henceforth, she would be a faithful believer in witchcraft. That lonely road looked like a haunt for gnomes, witches, and all the dread family of evil spirits."

In the midst of our conjectures and discussions the supper-bell rang, and I believe each of us felt some curiosity to see the newcomer. A slight-made young man, dressed in black, with a very intellectual face, stood conversing with our host in the supper-room, who introduced him to the company by the name of the Reverend Mr. Bennett. I exchanged a hasty glance with Cousin Tom; his conceit of a murdered traveller by such white clerical hands seemed so ridiculous that I could with much difficulty refrain from laughing, as I returned the gentleman's salutation. An hour was spent after supper in social conversation, when Mr. Bennett, pleading fatigue, retired for the night.

We immediately called the landlord to know if Mr. Bennett had mentioned having a companion with him.

"Yes; a friend of his had intended to have accompanied him to the Gap, but his horse had unfortuately fallen lame on the route, and he was for the present obliged to remain a short distance behind."

"But, where? where?" we all exclaimed.

"The gentleman did not mention where he had left his friend," but our host supposed about two miles below, opposite Columbia; the only stopping-place that he was aware of, near the Gap.

We did not think it expedient to tell him that we had seen both gentlemen not a mile from his hotel; and we thought it hardly probable that a traveller would journey two miles over one of the worst roads in Pennsylvania, to shelter a lame animal, when his stables were direct in his way, and not half the distance.

Long, that night, after we had sought our chambers, we conversed about the missing traveller. Josephine and myself shared the same room, and I was sitting at the window gazing down the road, now illuminated by the moonlight, when a sob from my companion made me start. She was standing by the dressing-table, reading a closely written note; so absorbed was she in her occupation, that she appeared unconscious of my presence; twice she perused the note through blinding tears; then, passionately kissing the paper, she threw herself on the bed in a paroxysm of grief. Surprised as well as alarmed by such a display of sorrow in one generally so cheerful, I approached, and throwing my arms around her begged her to be calm, and tell me the cause of such sudden distress.

"Oh, cousin! I cannot be calm," she exclaimed; "he is here."

"Who, dear Josa?"

"Henry," answered she, wildly gazing at me; "my Henry, whom I love better than life; he whom my father has forbidden me, on pain of his endless displeasure, to see or speak to again; and cousin," added she, with trembling lips, "I have solemnly promised to obey him;" and again she buried her sweet tearful face in the pillow. For some time she wept as if her heart were breaking; but, by degrees becoming more calm, she confided to me her "story of true love."

Her father, Mr. Gorden, was an eminent physician in Baltimore, in a successful practice of about ten thousand a year. He was one of those fortunate individuals with which our country abounds, who, by superior talents and industry, had risen from the middle ranks of life, to take an acknowledged station among the aristocracy of the land. Josephine was his idol; proud and overbearing to all the world beside, in the presence of his beautiful child his nature became softened to almost feminine tenderness. Her education and accomplishments had been his peculiar care; his indulgence towards her knew no bounds; the expensive presents he constantly lavished upon her silently attested how well he loved her; money was dross in his eyes compared to her happiness or enjoyment; yet, strange to relate, he had refused the hand of his daughter to Harry Le Roy, because he was not rich.

A gentleman, whose only recommendation was his immense wealth, was the suitor upon whom his choice fell. Married to him, Josephine's establishment would be of almost regal splendor, his ambitious dreams for her aggrandizement would be fully realized; and he still trusted that her filial affection and reverence for his wishes and opinions would prevail over the love she confessed for Le Roy; and in his proud imaginings he already beheld his darling girl the wife of the millionnaire.

Harry Le Roy had been dismissed with coldness and *hauteur*, that to one of his ardent temperament and Southern blood had been interpreted into a direct and deliberate insult. The bitterness of his outraged feelings had been increased by several letters that he had written to Josephine being returned unopened, and his being informed that she had left Baltimore to visit some relations in a distant State. No definite information could be obtained, and, wretched and hopeless, he had resorted to travel to deaden the misery of his mind.

By the merest chance, in Philadelphia, he obtained intelligence that she had accompanied a party of her relations in an excursion to the Delaware Water Gap. His resolution was instantly formed; he would follow her, see her, and learn his doom from her own lips.

The mystery was now solved. Harry Le Roy was the missing traveller. His tenderness for the feelings of Josephine would not permit him to appear before her unannounced; and he had remained in the solitary old house in the Gap, whilst his friend, Mr. Bennett, had preceded him to our hotel.

"Here, dearest Josephine," the note went on to say, "I await your decision; to me, it will be happiness or misery, life or death. The yearning love that fills my heart for you must be satisfied with a sight of that dear face. I feel that I cannot any longer exist without your presence. My Josephine; my beautiful, my own; yes, my own! for hearts that have been cemented like ours cannot be disunited by any earthly fiat. When and where we shall meet, I leave to you, my best beloved; but in a few hours I hope to hold you to a heart which, since we parted, has been filled with but one long thought of thee—only thee."

I confess, after reading this note, I never felt more perplexed in my life. I was some years older than Josephine, and I knew she would depend upon me for advice and assistance; but I also knew that her father would never forgive any interference with his commands; for the lovers to meet would be madness—but how was I to prevent it? After a few moments of troubled cogitation, I determined to remain neutral, and let things take their course. I knew that wicked urchin, Cupid, was not to be told, "Thus far shalt thou go, and no further;" and I foresaw that he intended to play some of his most mischievous pranks in this sequestered spot, that looked as if it had been expressly created to be the earthly Eden of his votaries. Josephine sat watching my countenance with breathless eagerness; she looked like a sculptured image, so pale and still. Gently lifting the dark ringlets that shaded her cheek, I softly kissed it; the electric chord of sympathy vibrated in each bosom, and without my uttering a word, she felt that I would aid and assist her; and, throwing herself on my bosom, she wept like a child. After much persuasion, I induced her to retire to rest; but her slumbers were broken and uneasy; she repeatedly murmured the name of her lover; and I saw, by the night-lamp, large tear-drops glistening on her fringed eyelids. Once, in supplicating accents, she exclaimed, "Father! dear father!" The next morning, Mr. Bennett proposed an excursion to Stroudsburg, a village a few miles distant from the Gap. Josephine, on the plea of a nervous headache, had not appeared at the breakfast-table; and when the rest of the party gladly acceded to his proposal, I excused myself as nurse to the invalid. Mr. Bennett gave me a quick glance of intelligence, and handing me a bouquet of wild roses, begged "I would present them, with his compliments, to Miss Gorden."

The carriages were soon at the door; and with many regrets that I could not go with them, to my great relief they departed. I immediately ascended to Josephine's chamber, and found her sitting by the window, quite calm and composed. In my absence, she had taken a sudden resolve to see Le Roy. "She would," she said, "tell him of the solemn promise her father had exacted from her; she would convince him it were better that they should not meet again; for the last time she would hear his voice and see his face. O!" continued she, with quivering accents, "situated as I now am, even my dear father would not object to this interview."

I had given her the bouquet of roses, and whilst speaking she had loosened the cord that bound them together, intending to arrange them in a china vase that stood on the table, when a small twisted note, that had been concealed in the centre of the bunch, fell to the floor; with a glowing cheek she raised it, saying, "O, this is so like Harry! How many bouquets of white camelias he used to send me! but in my eagerness to secure the dear little *billet doux* that I knew nestled inside, the poor flowers often perished."

She eagerly perused the well-known characters, and whilst she did so, her beautiful face became radiant with happiness. I never saw joy so vividly depicted on any other countenance.

"O, cousin!" she exclaimed, "he will be here in ten minutes, and I have not seen him for, ah, me! so many long months."

Tears of rapture glittered in her soft eyes, and she yielded herself to the delicious intoxication the certainty of seeing him again inspired, apparently thoughtless of all consequences. I will not portray their meeting, for Josephine insisted upon my being present. Theirs was no common attachment; every impulse of their souls was given to each other; few words were spoken, but as he held her to his heart, every feature proclaimed the victory of love. The hours to them seemed but minutes; and when at last, fearful of being surprised by our returning party, I gently hinted to him it was time to depart, he saucily told me "he did not intend to go at all." But at length, after Josephine promising him, if I would accompany her, to meet him in the afternoon, in the old road, a sequestered spot near a waterfall immediately beneath the Hotel, but by a steep bank of rocks completely concealed from observation, he consented to leave her.

She watched him, as he slowly paced along the road, until he was hidden from her sight; and then, for the first time, the thought was awakened in her mind, that she had broken the pledge she had given her father, and, contrary to his known command, was again about to hold a clandestine interview with her lover. The struggle in her mind was intense; her wounded conscience rebelled against her disobedience; she was distracted with contending emotions, for she was most tenderly attached to her father, who to her had ever been, except in this only instance, the most kind and indulgent of parents. But then, again, she had centred every hope of her life upon Le Roy. What should she do? Repel him—see him no more, forever? The thought had too much agony in it to be endured. No; she would meet him once more, and then they would part, and be to each other like the dead—only a memory!

Ah, delusive sophistry of a fond heart! The path of duty is a straight one; and he or she who deviates from its narrow track becomes bewildered in a labyrinth from which there is no return.

The old road, as it is called, now entirely disused, was shady and retired; it was close to the river's brink, and covered with a rich greensward, thickly gemmed with the blue forget-me-not; the same flowers so carefully cultivated in our gardens, which, in this mountain region, grow wild and abundant. A waterfall of considerable height fell over a precipice above, imparting a refreshing coolness to the air; huge rocks, of strange and irregular shapes, carpeted with thick moss, lay piled along the shore, forming luxurious resting-places for the loiterer. To this spot I accompanied Josephine to bid a last farewell to her lover. We had been now a week at the Gap, and our arrangements were already made to leave it the next day. As a turn in the road brought us in view of the cascade, we saw Le Roy standing with folded arms, leaning against the trunk of a huge sycamore tree, whose dense foliage threw a deep shadow across the path, broken by the golden sunshine piercing through its twisted branches into bright chequers on the verdant turf. Here, then,

> "Amidst the fall of waves, the fountain's gush,
> The sigh of winds, the music heard
> At eventide, from air and bush,
> The minstrelsy of leaf and bird,"

these two fond hearts, full of warm human love, met again, trusting in their own strength to part forever! I had seated myself on a shelving projection of rock that commanded a view of the river for some distance; my own heart was full of sad memories, phantoms of the things that were, and are not; and as I gazed upon the lovers, both so young and devoted, imaginations of Dryads and forest spirits, that in the olden time were thought to haunt the greenwood shade, stole over my senses, and I almost wished that from among the ancient trees around me some oracle would speak and divine their future!

Le Roy was a model of manly grace and beauty; he was reclining at Josephine's feet, drinking deep draughts of love from eyes whose tender glances told him, without the aid of words, how dear he was; they had been for some time conversing in low, earnest tones, he evidently pleading his passion, when Josephine called me to come to her, and, with much perturbation, informed me that she had consented to a secret marriage to take place that evening. It was in vain I remonstrated, and painted in vivid colors the folly of such a proceeding. I spoke of the anger of her father; the deceit she would be practising upon his fond and trusting affection; the remorse she must experience from such wilful disobedience to his wishes. I appealed to Le Roy's honor and generosity; but with Josephine's hand closely clasped in his own, he swore he never would resign her but with life. The very name of Mr. Gorden appeared to awaken all the angry passions of his nature; he said he had wronged and insulted him; that in his wanton pride he had sought to crush the affections of both their hearts, and offer up his daughter a sacrifice at the shrine of mammon. Josephine pleaded for her father, and bitterly wept, but it was upon her lover's bosom. She seemed to be surrounded by a magnetic spell that she was unable to break; all her resolves had melted away before the impassioned eloquence of Le Roy. Before we had left the spot, moved by her tears and entreaties, I had pledged myself to silence and secrecy, and promised to be a witness of their nuptials. It was arranged to take place at midnight, in the old house at the Gap. Mr. Bennett, who had been in orders for some years, was to perform the ceremony.

Le Roy was not to claim her as his wife for one year; and, in the meantime, Josephine trusted to soften her father's prejudices, and, in some favorable moment, to reveal to him her disobedience, and to be forgiven.

The clock in the dining-room had told the hour of twelve. The full moon shone with unclouded lustre, as with noiseless steps we left the portico of the hotel. I gave a searching glance at the windows of the chambers, but the white curtains were closely drawn, and the deep stillness that reigned through the mansion convinced me that we had nothing to fear from the prying eyes of curiosity. I thought Mr. Bennett seemed more agitated than Josephine; not a word was spoken by either of us. A few yards from the house, emerging from the shadow of a tree near the spring, we met Le Roy. In silence he folded Josephine to his breast, and pressed a kiss upon her cheek, that I saw by the moonlight was as pale as marble!

Arrived at the house, we were met by the old man and his wife, the only occupants of that solitary dwelling; they had, of necessity, been taken into our confidence. On a table in the small parlor, over which a dip candle shed a ghostly light, I observed an Episcopal prayer-book, opened at the ordinance of marriage. All Josephine's firmness seemed to forsake her at the sight of these preparations, and she sank half-fainting on a chair.

There was a dread, an awe upon my own spirit, as if some misfortune was lowering over us; I tried to shake off the ominous feeling, and inspire the trembling girl with the courage I needed myself, but in vain; and as the solemn words were pronounced, so pregnant with the happiness or misery of her future life, I thought I heard the slow tolling of a bell, as if for a soul just departed! The measured tones fell upon my ear with such distinctness that it was difficult for me to convince myself that it was a delusion of my excited senses.

Le Roy insisted upon accompanying us to the door of the hotel, where he took a passionate farewell of his bride; and without accident or interruption we regained our chambers. As I pressed my throbbing head on the pillow, I could scarce believe that the events of the last few hours were not the illusions of a distempered dream. Josephine, exhausted by such unwonted excitement, was soon wrapt in profound slumber. She never appeared more touchingly lovely in my eyes: her cheek, reposing upon an arm that looked as if it were chiselled from marble, was flushed to the hue of a ripe pomegranate; her rich dark hair in graceful ringlets lay in disordered confusion on her brow and bosom; a smile yet lingered upon her lips, and a childlike purity and beauty was beaming from every lineament of her sweet face. And, alas! she, now slumbering so tranquilly there, had taken the destiny of her life in her own hands. A sickness of the heart oppressed me as I asked myself the momentous question—would it be for good or for evil?

The next morning, while the mists were climbing up the sides of the mountains in many fantastic shapes, we left the Water Gap.

On arriving in Philadelphia, we found Mr. Gorden awaiting his daughter. The father met his child with delighted affection; she sprang towards him and hid her face on his shoulder, and I feared the excess of her emotion would arouse his suspicions. Her open and guileless nature shrank appalled from the task she had imposed upon it. Hitherto, there had been entire confidence between them; now, in the hidden recesses of her heart there lay a dread secret in which that dear father must not participate. I foresaw that, with her quick sensibilities, ere long all would be revealed.

They returned to Baltimore, and, six months afterwards, I received a letter from Josephine, beseeching me to come to her; she said "that her life was a burden too heavy to be borne; the deceit she was hourly practising upon a parent, whose every thought was for her happines, was preying upon her health. Her alarmed and anxious father was constantly heaping upon her manifestations of his affection, and devising some new scheme of pleasure to divert her mind; but this only increased the remorse of her spirit. Le Roy, too, forgetful of his promises made at the Gap, was anxious to claim her as his wife; he pleaded the sufferings he endured in hearing vague reports of her indisposition, and being unable to approach her; he said it was impossible for him, situated as they now were, to pursue his profession with any success; that with the absorbing love that filled his very being for her, he could no longer consent to this separation, and live.

There remained, then, no alternative but to hasten to Baltimore, and declare the position of Josephine to Mr. Gorden. I found the sweet girl looking harassed and careworn. For several days, our minds were much engaged in what manner we should reveal her marriage to her father. At length it was arranged that I should be the person to communicate the intelligence; it was an agitating task, and fearful that my courage would completely fail me, if it were any longer deferred, I sought an interview that afternoon with Mr. Gorden.

I was ushered into a large and well-filled library, fitted up with all the appliances that wealth can command, or luxury desire. He was a fine-looking old gentleman of about sixty-seven, bland and courteous in his manners, with all the refinement and polish of the "old school," as it is now termed. He received me with much politeness, and ordering the servant to place a chair for me, begged me to be seated. My heart beat almost audibly. He observed my agitation, and tried to dispel it, by producing from a small rosewood box a magnificent set of pearls he had purchased that morning, as a birth-day present for his darling daughter. I felt still more oppressed by this communication. I dreaded the revulsion of feeling he would experience when I had made known my mission; for a moment I hesitated; but I concluded it was more advisable to impart my intelligence at once than to defer it to some other period.

In as few words as possible, I told my story; but I had not estimated its effects upon Mr. Gorden. The treachery of his daughter seemed more terrible to him than death itself; his countenance became fearfully convulsed; he arose from his seat, his face livid with passion, and raising his clenched hands above his head, he imprecated a fearful curse upon Josephine and her husband. A moment more, and, struck with paralysis, he lay like a ghastly corpse at my feet.

For some weeks, Mr. Gorden lingered in a critical situation; all access to his chamber was strictly forbidden by his physicians. Josephine's agony and remorse may be imagined, but not described; she had not seen her father since the fatal hour in which I had revealed her disobedience. He was now pronounced convalescent. The first words he uttered, were to inquire if his daughter was yet an inmate of his house? On being answered in the affirmative, he sent her his commands to leave it, and forever! He ordered her wardrobe, and all articles belonging to her, to be packed up and sent to her address; he commanded a beautiful full-length portrait of her, by Inman, to be taken from the drawing-room; and forbade any member of his household ever to name or allude to her in his presence: he said, from henceforth he had no daughter—Josephine no father!

Two days thence, the heart-stricken girl and her husband were on the way to the South. There, in the bosom of the Le Roy family, as the wife of their darling Harry, "the winds of heaven were not suffered to visit her cheek too roughly," and she experienced all the kindness and affection her gentleness and beauty were so calculated to inspire. Idolized by her husband, who seemed each day to become more devoted to her; every effort that the fondest love could devise, to make her forget the past, was resorted to by him; and, to the superficial observer, her cup of happiness appeared full; but there was one drop whose bitterness poisoned the draught. Remembrances of her father, left desolate in his old age; of that happy home, where so much indulgence had been lavished upon her, now closed against her forever, thronged upon her mind. The present was lost in the past; she yearned with painful longings to throw herself upon the breast that had nurtured her childhood; she pined for the forgiveness she feared would never be accorded to her.

Letter after letter had been written to her incensed parent, and had been returned with the seals unbroken.

Before her husband and his family, Josephine never uttered one repining word; but, alone with her God, she prayed for the pardon of the sin, whose consequences were blighting her young life.

Her situation quickened her sensibilities to the sacredness of the tie between parent and child; and when the thought intruded itself that her sacrilegious hand had broken that holy bond; that her guilty disobedience was perhaps bringing her father's gray hairs in sorrow to the grave, the remorse of her wrung spirit was almost beyond her endurance.

I had received several letters from her since her residence in Charleston, and in the last she had written to me she complained of severe indisposition. Anxious to hear tidings of her, one evening, when the same party that had accompanied her to the Delaware Water Gap were again assembled together, I sent to the post-office. A letter was handed to me, bearing the Charleston post-mark; on opening it, I found it was from Le Roy's mother, stating, "that three days previous, Josephine had died in her first accouchement!"

Silence and dust on that beautiful brow! How could we realize an affliction so sudden and overwhelming? "How many hopes were borne upon thy bier, oh, bride of stricken love!"

The sad intelligence was abruptly communicated to Mr. Gorden; a second attack of paralysis was the result; and in a few weeks the broken-hearted old man was laid beside his daughter!

In the Cemetery at Baltimore, as you enter the south gate, a monument of chaste and exquisite design arrests your attention. Reposing on a broad slab of Italian marble is an urn, wreathed with a light and graceful foliage of leaves and flowers; the emblems are a torch reversed and a rose-bud broken—symbols of Love and Death.

Beneath this is simply inscribed the name of Josephine!

EASTON, PA., 1841.

Passage of the Blue Ridge at the Delaware Water Gap.

BY DR. WILLIAM B. DEY.

Huge pile of Nature's majesty! how oft
The mind, in contemplation wrapt, has scann'd
Thy form serene and naked; if to tell,
That when creation from old chaos rose,
Thou wert as now thou art; or if some cause,
Some secret cause, has rent thy rocky mantle,
And hurl'd thy fragments o'er the plain below.
The pride of man may form conceptions vast,
Of all the fearful might of giant power
That rent the rampart to its very base,
Giving an exit to Lenape's stream,
And wildly mixing with woods and waters.
A mighty scene to set enchantment free,
Burst the firm barrier of eternal rock,
If by the howling of volcanic rage,
Or foaming terror of Noachian floods.
Let fancy take her strongest flight; she ne'er
Can reach the state of primoidal things,
As darkness brooded o'er the deep abyss;
Where at the fiat of Eternal might.
E'en the vast fabric of our planet Earth,
Arose most beauteous from its Maker's hand,
With flower, plant, and noble oak o'erspread,
And made the dwelling-place of man himself,
In form majestic, but in soul a god.
But, as for us, let speculations go,
And be the food of geologic sons;
Who from the pebble judge the mountain's form,
And oft the structure of this dark terrene.
Most all abstractionists assign a cause,
If cause it be, for all created things;

And in their wisdom dive into the deep,
Or search the secret of the carbon mine;
Or scan the structure of a human skull,
To prove the essence of the thought within;
Whilst to their minds, thus wrapt in darkness deep,
The sun of light affords no ray of knowledge.
Apart from these we'll carry on our theme,
The wild and fearful pass, whose grandeur speaks
A language known to every fearful eye;
Breathing enchantment through the very bosom.
Here was the home of Nature's hardy sons,
The freeborn dwellers of their native soil.
They had no equal—they were Nature's chief—
Mighty; magnanimous. But where are they?
Let echo answer, where! The earth can tell
A long sad tale of desolate despair,
The broken mound, and moss-clad stone at best,
Denote the spot where Indian grandeur sleeps.
All else is still; a death-shade to the mind;
The land of woe, of dark forgetfulness.
The white man came with plunder on his wings,
With cursed love of gold—hypocrisy—
And e'en the Cross, outstretch'd before his arms,
To bring destruction on this happy race,
And make a waste of all their fatherland.
The mountain bird, the emblem of the free,
Wild as old ocean in his boundless range,
Here held his empire free at will to roam.
Praise be to thee, thou monarch of the winds:
However humble be the strain I give,
Yet still to thee, thou king of native plumes!
I willing give the off'ring of my heart.

Lo! my eyrie I form, far, far away,
  On the mountain's rocky crest;
The eaglet securely reposes there,
  In his wild and moss-bound nest.

There, the wild tempest's rage disturbs it not,
 For, lo! 'tis the place of the free;
And the nightwind's moan, as it passes by,
 Is a dulcet-tone to thee.

The lightning's flash, and the thunder's sound,
 That shakes the stern mountain form,
Securely leave the bleak eyrie there,
 Untouched by the wrath of the storm.

The warrior chief, as he hastened by
 In pursuit of the flying deer,
Found not the home of the monarch bird,
 On his mountain crag so drear.

A health to thee of the crested form,
 Thou pride of a nation's land!
May the foeman that aims a blow at thee,
 Lie low as his broken brand!

Forever perch on the mast of the brave,
 Forever be 'mid the fight,
When the sulphury smoke on the blast rides high,
 And the warrior tries his might.

What are the monuments of art, compared
To nature's varied forms? Lenape's pass,
Where flows the Delaware in silent pride,
As if well conscious of his mighty name,
Will ever claim the freeman's honest praise.
The gorgeous temple that proud prelates reared,
Drawn by the genius of an Angelo;
The moss-grown monuments of Palenque;
The mighty structures of the plain of Thebes;
The hundred columns of Persepolis;
The Hindoo works among the rocks of Goa,
Or Trajan's pillar on the banks of Tiber,
Alike attest the wondrous art of man.

But nature's self appears! Her majesty
Bewilders every thought, and loud proclaims
The hand of Deity in all her works.
Through nature we can look to nature's God,
If in the zephyr, or the whirlwind blast;
The green savanna, or the burning desert;
The foam of ocean, or the forest wood;
The purling stream, or wild Lenape's form;
The ragged rocks, majestic, bold, and grand;
That rear their frowning battlements on high,
Where glides the glassy stream of Delaware,
The stranger's heart with ecstasy will fill,
Till Time himself shall slumber on his car,
And darkness reign amid the vast profound.

Lost on the Mountain.

The early autumn days in the country are the loveliest of the year: an atmosphere not yet obscured by the haze of Indian summer, yet so cool and invigorating, that rambling over hills and climbing rugged summits, so tiresome in the sultry days of summer, are now delightful employments.

Though the bright flowers of spring have withered on the frail stem, and the richer profusion of summer varieties are faded and falling, autumn fields are arrayed in a wealth of orange, purple, and gold, peculiarly their own. The outer foliage is tipped with the same rich hues, whilst the forest itself still retains the vernal bloom of summer days. Ferns have attained their perfection of growth and beauty, and the mosses, the never changing, ever beautiful mosses, offer their humble tribute, alike to autumn, spring, summer, and winter.

A rare enjoyment was afforded the visitors at the Water Gap on one of the lovely days of this season, in the autumn of 1867.

At its close the guests were assembled at the supper-table, each relating his own adventures, the discoveries made, and the enjoyments experienced. The name of one was mentioned who was observed by several during the afternoon as untiring, and who seemed to have visited almost every place of interest within reach of the day's excursion.

Gifted to a high degree, refined and cultivated, she found a multitude of objects for admiration and study: the mountain brook passing stealthily by in suppressed murmurings, or roaring and foaming over cascades and through wild ravines, is equally musical; the verdure-clad rocks are not passed by unheeded, nor the trees, in their varied form and beauty, some grown gray in years, and from whose wide-spreading branches the mosses hang their silken tassels, and adorn the venerable trunk with crimson and frosted coraline.

It was not a surprise that this lady did not appear first, at the evening meal, but when not found in her room, some anxiety began to be felt.

She had been last seen by a returning party, near Prospect Rock, and though she expressed a desire to witness the setting sun from the summit of Mount Minsi, they did not suppose she would undertake the journey alone at that late hour.

The supper is finished in silence. The sun is sinking deep behind the western hills. The chirping of winged insects in the over-hanging trees, always most welcome, now speak too plainly of coming night. The evening is chill and uncomfortable. The dew is falling, and darkness has thrown her mantle over the broad face of nature, closing the scene of an enchanting day, and leaving the drama of the night to be performed in darkness.

All eyes are directed to the mountains. How dark and how solitary they appear! Can it be that a lonely female is wandering in those gloomy shadows, over ragged rocks, through tangled woods and broken ravines! Darker still grows the night and she does not appear! The alarm has become wide-spread, and among the ladies

> . . . . "There was hurrying to and fro,
> And gathering tears, and tremblings of distress."

Stalwart men are collecting in numbers from the village, and propose to organize with the guests of the Hotel for a thorough exploration of the mountain. Companies are formed and sections apportioned.

All is hurry and confusion amid the din of preparation, but in half an hour signal guns are heard echoing along the mountain side and through the gorge. Fires are kindled on every prominence. How they glow and sparkle and roar, and how beautifully the bright blaze jets forth in eccentric currents, rising high in the still air, lighting up the tall old trees, and picturing ghostly shadows against the face of the pinnacled rocks. But how wonderfully circumscribed the extent of the illumination; the brilliant coruscations but make the blackness of night visible, and deepen the gloom of its shadows beyond.

The inmates of a few scattered dwellings along the base of the mountain are aroused from their early slumbers by a party sent in that direction. In answer to the inquiries about the lost lady, one of them had heard cries in the thicket further up the mountain, which sounded like some one in distress. He had called, but the cry then ceased, and he concluded it was a "painter."

These tidings gave painful apprehensions to those who did not know the story was pure fiction, and manufactured for the benefit of "city people."

The "thicket," however, is diligently searched, with silent forebodings of the fate of the lady in this dismal, tangled woods, while some, entertaining a more selfish view of the situation, are shuddering at the thought of a panther dropping suddenly upon them from an overhanging tree.

A returning party from the summit at 10 o'clock give no encouragement to the anxious numbers collected and in waiting at the foot of the mountain.

They had reached the end of the pathway, and should the lady, in the darkness, have attempted to go further, or, by accident have fallen upon the loose stones of the descending slope, she must have gone down and over the precipice, and we could only expect to find her mangled body on the projecting rocks hundreds of feet below. None are disposed to entertain this fearful conjecture, but more willing to conclude she must still be on the north side of the mountain.

The night is growing colder. If she has fallen or become disabled, she must perish before morning. Eagerly the search is continued. Every thicket in which she might be deliriously wandering, and every known cliff from which she might have fallen, is thoroughly examined.

A party is now sent to explore the ravine from "The Hunter's Spring" to "Eureka." And whilst this search is in progress, let us turn to what was really transpiring, as subsequently revealed.

After her friends had left her, the lady entered the open pathway leading up the mountain. Her impulse to follow it was irresistible. She had over two hours of daylight, and could readily reach the summit and return to the Hotel at a seasonable hour.

She is now in the forest and alone, but

not in solitude, for she communes with a multitude that speak the language and poetry of nature, with which her soul is in sweet harmony. She hears the winds, that have been sighing through the branches of these stately forest trees for a century, still croaking the melancholy tale heard by the red man with sad forebodings of his own unhappy fate, when he rested wearily under its shadows.

Eureka's gurgling source, in concert with the music of the woods, grows wild, but not discordant, when from far down the ravine comes up the loud laughter of its foaming waters.

Hard by is a little grotto, with its moss-covered floor. How inviting it looks! She cannot resist resting a moment on its rocky parapet. How gracefully the rhododendrons bend over the fairy little chamber to afford a perpetually cooling archway! The ferns stoop to kiss the tiny waters that ooze from the side of the grotto and trickle down the face of the rocks, like joyful tear-drops down the cheeks of a happy maiden.

Near the grotto lies the trunk of a great old tree. The hand of man long since stripped it of its own covering and left it naked to the elements. She pauses to witness how lovingly the mosses have entwined it, re-clothing its weather-stained form with their own "silken verdure," and how beautified it appears in its green old age. But the little germs of kindred trees already growing upon its ruined body, and taking nourishment from its decaying fibres, speak of its speedy dissolution, and nature's generous effort to replace the fallen monarch, and restore the forest to its wonted beauty.

Further on piles of huge rocks appear, covered with great sheets of velvet lichen, now, during the dry season, parched and rolled, but when moistened again, spread themselves over the granite surface, to commence life's struggle anew. What instructive lessons the mosses and lichens teach us! Was ever so much beauty joined with such humility? Yet we step aside from our own pathway to trample on the tapestried mound, and ruthlessly destroy in a thoughtless moment, the accumulated beauty and growth of a century; not discerning that,

"The tiny moss, whose silken verdure clothes
The time-worn rock, and whose bright capsules rise,

Like fairy urns on stalks of golden sheen,
Demand our admiration and our praise,
As much as cedar kissing the blue sky,
Or Krubuls' giant flower. God made them all,
And what *He* deigns to make, should ne'er be deem'd
Unworthy of our study and our love."

Our lady friend, though lingering long in her communings with nature, gained the rugged summit in season to witness the glory of the sun's declining rays resting on the crest of the opposite mountain.

It is not surprising that her mind was greatly absorbed in the contemplation of a scene like this. At this hour of the day the effect produced upon the commonest observer, is one of wonder and admiration. To her, it was positive enchantment. It awakened, too, the memories of her far-off mountain home. In imagination she is dwelling again in the highlands, surrounded by familiar objects, familiar faces, and receiving pleasant greetings.

She heeds not the passing moments, and is only awakened from her reverie by the shades of night falling gloomily upon the enchanting scene. Arousing herself and feeling chilled by the falling dew, she starts rapidly on her return to the Hotel, three miles away.

No fear has yet come upon her. She has the confidence acquired amid loftier ranges in her native mountains, and feels she can accomplish the journey without fear or fatigue. Once upon the open path she can keep it without difficulty.

Proceeding but a short distance, however, she sees, or imagines she sees, a man approaching. She steps aside from the path in the thick bushes to avoid being seen. Strange it is, that in solitary places, we are so much startled, and for a moment affrighted in coming suddenly in presence of beings like ourselves, though we may not "stand in *awe* of such a *thing*," in the sense used by Shakspeare.

In attempting to regain the pathway, it is supposed she took the opposite direction, and is soon wandering wearily through the wild woods, and in darkness, and for the first time fear comes upon her,—*she is lost.*

Those only who have had the experience can understand the strange hallucination of mind produced by being lost on a cloudy day in the woods, and to what a painful degree this delirium is increased when occurring at night and in a strange locality. It will be impossible for any one without this experience to comprehend the suffering condition of this young lady.

To be lost is, for the time, to be *non compos mentis.* If one reasons at all, his reasoning is upon false premises, and as to conclusions, he never arrives at any, or if he imagines he does, he has too little faith in his own perverted judgment to adopt them. He is at sea without chart or compass, and with a novice at the helm. The position of every object he sees or comes in contact with is reversed. The hills, the rocks, the trees, and all the landmarks with which he may have been once familiar, are familiar no longer; they are changed, and the direction they point to is not the one his judgment inclines him to follow.

The friendly light in the distant cottage is a star in the firmament. Even the streams flow in contrary directions, and he feels a little staggered to see for the first time, water running *up hill;* but he knows it does, as well as he knows where he is, and if he could place sufficient confidence in anything to swear by, he would be willing to make the declaration.

Neither is he exactly sure that the ground he stands upon is *terra firma*, for it certainly *swims*, and as to the conformation of the earth's surface, there is a monstrous delusion about it somehow, for there is no level land nor descending grade, but the whole thing is an "up-hill business." He wanders about, never going straightforward, but travelling a mile or two in the direction he wishes to go, finds himself presently at the place of starting, slightly irritated and a little discomposed. Again and again he makes the trial, with the same unfortunate results, until at last he begins seriously to discuss that most difficult of all questions, his own sanity.

He finds it impossible to settle satisfactorily this knotty question, but remains as much in doubt as to what step next to take to extricate himself from his unpleasant dilemma, when he sits down quietly, and philosophically resolves to "wait for something to turn up."

The young lady, bewildered and in darkness, is wandering in the same toilsome weary round, fearful to rest, and yet suffering increasing terrors at every advancing footstep. All the sounds of the never-silent woods, the croaking vibrations of the tall trees, whose pinnacled branches catch the current of the passing winds, which made sweet music an hour ago, now send forth dismal sighs and unearthly moanings.

Spectral shadows dance before her, darker than the forest gloom of night. The rustling of the leaves produced by her own weary tread, startle her, and she almost feels the fearful touch of some pursuing monster.

From the summit runs a slope at a sharp angle to the edge of the precipice, covered with loose rocks and stones, detached from the crest by the frosts of many winters; along the edge of this precipice grow a few stunted trees, receiving precarious nourishment from earth filling the deep fissures in its exposed surface.

As the tired deer through the thick forest by yelping hounds long pursued, leaves its only place of security and flies recklessly to the open plain, exposing itself to new and untried dangers, so this lady, pursued by her own desperate fears, and seeking relief from the terror of the woods, coming at length in view of the open space, runs hurriedly out upon the rocky slope, and in a moment is carried down struggling with the moving mass to the edge of the precipice, and frantically clasps a tree, providentially in position to save her from impending destruction.

She does not at first realize the peril of her new situation, but for a moment experiences a sense of relief in having escaped from what her harassed mind was no longer capable of enduring. She can now see the stars in the broad expanse of heaven, and a ray of comfort is afforded her in the welcome light from a few scattered dwellings far below her along the margin of the river. In the dark woods she feared the sound of her own breathing, but now, for the first time, calls loudly for assistance. Too far below the summit for those to hear who were in search on the north side, and yet too high for the sound to strike the dwellings nearest the base of the mountain, she continues her cries with the full strength of her lungs for long, weary hours, but without any evidence that she is either heard or regarded. Her voice at length grows weak, and her frame is becoming exhausted, but her mind is fully alive to the hopelessness of her condition. Her life depended upon keeping the exact position in which she found herself placed. She could move neither to the right nor left. Behind her the treacherous rocks were ready to move with a touch and carry her over the precipice; before her, the yawning chasm. She could never wish herself back in those terrifying woods, yet she realizes now that her last condition is worse than the first.

O! the agony, the fearfully protracted, the momentarily increasing agony of these despairing hours! "Will no one hear me?" "Will no one come to my relief?" "Hope is dying within me; I must perish here, and alone?"

Still clinging to the tree, she endeavors to write upon her tablet an account of her situation. Her whole life passes in review before her. Her home and the cherished associations of her childhood. One by one she calls her friends and kindred by name, and gives to each a lasting farewell, and in prayer commits her soul to God.

At about the hour of eleven a messenger arrives at the Hotel, with the joyful intelligence that the cries of the lady had been heard on the south side of the mountain, and that two men had gone to her rescue. But can they reach her from that direction?

The men were hardy and strong, and familiar with every pass. None knew better than they the hazardous nature of the enterprise they were about to engage in, but none more able nor more willing to execute it. An irregular circuitous journey of at least three miles must be performed before reaching that portion of the summit.

They shout as they clamber along the base of the cliff, and she indistinctly hears the joyful signal, which gives her the first gleam of hope she has experienced in her long painful captivity. As they recede along the side of the mountain the sound of their voices die away, and she hears it no longer. She feels now that she has been but mocked and is abandoned to her fate, and the hope of rescue, entertained for a moment, is succeeded by an overwhelming despondency. Her aching arms still cling to the friendly tree, but she feels she can retain her precarious position but a little while longer. The suffering cold, long endured, is now producing a stupefying drowsiness, against which she struggles with all the power of her strong will, well knowing that one moment's sound unconscious sleep would loosen her hold, and then all would soon be over. But how hard to resist this imperative demand of nature! If she could only move about, she might overcome the stupor, but she is a captive, held by flaming daggers bristling on every side. There is but one little spot upon all the broad earth on which her feet are permitted to rest. That dreadful sensation of falling from giddy heights, which we sometimes experience in our dreams, is fearfully magnified during one of these drowsy intervals, but the horrible sensation produced, assists her in rallying to wakeful consciousness.

She looks up to the stars of heaven no longer, and the glimmering lights in the distant cottages flicker, faint, and die. Her dearest friends are but dim shadows in her fast-fading recollection, and the busy world, with all its beauties and its joys, is receding from her memory, and forever disappearing.

There is at this moment floating upon the still air, the far-off sound of human voices, whether dreaming, she knows not, but it is soothing balm to her weary, sick soul. Nearer as it approaches becomes the consciousness of its reality. Her ear is growing alive to the welcome music. Louder and more distinct appears the sound, and surely approaching. O! what joyful tidings,—it is the call of the two faithful, trusty men!

"Thank heaven my prayers are answered!
I live to see my rescue, and my reason is not dethroned!"

The chilled, almost lifeless body, is revitalized, and to the weakness of a child is imparted, in a moment, the wonted strength and firmness of a hero.

So much has the mind a controlling influence over the body, that it is fair to presume that one less highly cultivated, logical, and vigorous in intellect, with a body of twice the strength of her own, would scarcely have survived this terrible ordeal.

It will be remembered, that, in the expedition of Lieutenant Strain across the Isthmus, the able-bodied laboring men, with the average lack of intellectual culture of their class, were the first to yield to the hard necessities of their situation, and the first to miserably perish; whilst the Lieutenant, with the physician and two or three engineers, men of high order of culture, each of whom performed twice the amount of his share of labor, and endured a greater amount of privation from hunger, were the only ones of the party who survived the rigors of that terrible campaign.

The two men had now gained the summit, but at what toil and fearful risk of life, can only be understood by an examination of their route. Few men would be willing to make the ascent by daylight. They came along the edge of the summit, avoiding a too near approach to the sliding rocks, and at length arrived at the point where they expected to find the lady; but they were horrified on hearing the answer to their call, to find that she was far below them and on the very verge of the precipice. They did not, however, need to offer her words of assurance or encouragement; she was herself again, and felt that whatever of fortitude or courage might be required in the accomplishment of her rescue, she was disciplined for the work.

For the first time the men found themselves at fault. They needed now what seemed indispensable to her rescue—*a rope.* With it, one of the men could easily let himself down the rocky slope, and support himself by it in bearing up the precious burden. But no time was to be lost. They returned a short distance on the brow of the mountain, and found a place of easy descent to the crest, along which they passed with cautious steps, steadying themselves by support received from each other, and an occasional tree or twig, until they arrived near that most fearful position, where the moving mass of rocks had crowded on the edge of the precipice. She hears the cautious movements of the men, and gives kind encouraging words to their generous exertions. They are now almost within reach of her, yet fearing to take another step lest they set in motion the treacherous mass, and all be carried down together; but they must pass over to her, or she to them. She will listen but to the one suggestion: she is willing and anxious to make the trial. She swings herself round the tree, one dexterous sprightly leap upon the angry rocks,—a second bound with fairy lightness,—a third, and she is safe in the hands of her rescuers. She scarcely needs assistance in following the footsteps of the men along the edge of the dangerous cliff. They gain the narrowed slope, which she ascends with the proffered aid of the men, and once more stands securely on the summit of Mount Minsi, grateful beyond the power of language to express.

The three miles' walk to the Hotel is accomplished easily and expeditiously, where she arrives at one o'clock in the morning; fervently acknowledges the earnest congratulations of the anxious joyous multitude in waiting, walks firmly on to her chamber, and falls fainting on the floor.

HISTORICAL.

Sketch of the Minisink and its Early People.

FROM the earliest intercourse of our ancestors with the aboriginal inhabitants, that portion of the Delaware situated north of the Blue Ridge or Kittatinny Mountain, has been known as the *Minisink*. It properly comprises all the territory north of the mountain—up to an uncertainly defined limit—drained by the river Delaware and its tributaries. We speak of it, however, as that portion adjacent to the river and the valley lands of its branches, near their confluence with the Delaware. Its extent up the river is not definitely fixed. It is sometimes spoken of as terminating at the Naversink, then at the mouth of the Lackawaxen, while others contend that the name embraced the whole of the upper valley of the Delaware.

The signification of the word "Minisink" is said to be, *the water is gone.* There is little authority in proof of this definition, and that only traditional, hence it will always be entertained with much doubt. There seems, however, to be *no doubt* that there was such a tradition, and if the wonderful phenomenon of the bursting asunder of the mountain at the Water Gap, and the sudden disappearance of a lake of such magnitude as must have then existed, occurred at any time during which the natives occupied this portion of the country, it would have been an event of such moment as to cause its ready transmission from generation to generation, down to the period of their intercourse with the European settlers.*

* The tradition was that long ago, and before the Delaware broke through the mountain at the Water Gap, these lands, for thirty or forty miles along it, were covered by a lake, but became drained by the breaking down of that part of the dam which confined it. And the people who lived upon the lands from which the water had retired were called "Minsies," because they lived upon land from which the water had gone.

The name in the first instance was descriptive of the land, and afterwards applied to the Indians who lived upon it.—*Eager's History of Orange County.*

The wonderful action of the aqueous element in this valley is abundantly evident. It is visible on the sides of the mountain, as well as in the valleys and table lands. Conical-shaped hills, such as are so prominent in Shaw's meadows, in Cherry Valley, and the sand-hills near the mouth of the Bushkill, are to be seen all through the Minisink.

These diluvial cones are not composed of the surrounding material, nor are they like the eternal hills in their inner structure, but a mass of pebbles and sand from base to apex, with an occasional well-rounded boulder; proving conclusively the action of water in their formation. There is also evidence of *glacial action* in the *striated* and *furrowed* rocks in place. All theories, however, of the formation of the passage of the Delaware through the mountain are in doubt, and to each are presented obstacles which the light of science may or may not hereafter remove. The whole valley presents an interesting field for geological investigation, and is studded with beautiful landscape pictures.

In this valley, and among these mountains, or perhaps on the borders of the Great Lake, once dwelt a branch of the ancient *Lenni Lenape* nation, known as the *Minsi* tribe. For how many centuries their "council fires" were lighted on the margin of these waters, we shall perhaps never know with any degree of certainty.

The "Minsis" were distinguished not only for their valor, when that quality was brought into requisition, but equally distinguished for honesty and integrity. It appears really wonderful to those who have inquired closely into the character of these simple-minded dwellers of the forest, how many they possessed of those nobler traits of character which adorn civilized life, and how much more exalted a sense of Deity they entertained than is ordinarily manifested in savage nations. "They worshipped a spirit whom they called the *Great Mannitto*, which answers to our sacred word God or Creator, and who, though invisible, was recognized as the great First Cause."

After all we have heard in general derogation of the character of the North American Indians, we should be almost incredulous at this evidence of the intuitive perception on the part of the Lenapes, of that which not only the light of civilization, but the sacred truths of Divine Revelation seem scarcely sufficient to inspire in the minds of enlightened nations, were it not derived from sources we cannot question. And it appears, also, that they were to a remarkable degree susceptible to the impressive teachings of such men as David and John Brainerd, Heckewelder, Ziesberger, and others; and that the light of Christian civilization for which they seemed to be yearning was already beginning to dawn.

But it is melancholy to contemplate, that the good seed sown by these earnest and zealous men, after giving signs of a permanent growth and the promise of a fruitful harvest, should be trodden under and almost eradicated by others, professing to believe in and be governed by the same Christian precepts, but whose conduct showed them to the poor Indians to be more vile and wicked than the most abandoned of their own people. Whose sole object appeared to be, to cheat them of their lands, destroy their humble habitations, and, finally, to exterminate the race.

The missionary labors among the Lenapes were at first attended with good results. The Moravians established their mission at Bethlehem, in 1742, and David Brainerd commenced his labors at Crosswicks, in New Jersey, the year following.

There was an Indian village in Cherry Valley not far from the Wind Gap, which the Moravians visited by invitation in 1747. The place was called *Miniolagameka* (meaning a spot of rich land amidst that which is barren).

Besides the mission-house at Bethlehem, the Moravians had various stations throughout the Delaware, Lehigh, and Susquehanna Valleys. There was a station at Dunsbury (Stroudsburg), on the west side of Brodhead's Creek, near the iron bridge; and one at Walpack in the Minisink.

The mission at Bethlehem was visited in one year by 800 different Indians.

The first one baptized was *Joshua*, in 1742. He lived a Christian life and died in 1775. He was an assistant in the missionary work, and was the instrument of much good among his people. After our Indians were driven first to the Susquehanna and then to the

West, Joshua labored among them at their settlement near Pittsburg.

It appears very wonderful to us who live in this progressive age, that these people, endowed with many capacities and who seemed to be on the very verge of civilization, should have remained for hundreds and perhaps thousands of years, without approaching any nearer; doing just what their fathers did and nothing more. No one mighty mind to break the frail trammels that bound him to the dusky past, and soaring high above the rest, lift the thin veil that shut out from his vision the light of intellectual day.

Does it not teach us that there is no real progress in the human races, outside of the influences of the Christian religion, and a recognition of the truths of the Bible? The wild Arabs of to-day are those of long centuries past. As they were seen and known then, we see them and know them now—still groping in the dark, still wandering in the desert.

There seems to be no doubt that these Indians desired to live on terms of friendship with the white settlers; they evidently looked upon them as a superior order of beings, and, at first, thinking to be made wiser and better by their teaching and example, they were made welcome, so far as the simple native manners of these people could testify.

Could we have more conclusive evidence of the friendly disposition of the Minsis, than is derived from the fact, that for more than half a century they lived quietly and peaceably with the white settlers in this valley, and permitted them to cut down their forests and cultivate their best hunting grounds, all unprotected as the confiding settlers were, against their overpowering numbers, and the means they possessed of exterminating them without warning, should they be disposed at any time to do so!

Yet, in all this long period of years, we hear of the commission of no single act of violence on the part of the Indians. And when the general outbreak occurred in 1755, those who had dealt fairly and honorably with them, were as secure in their persons and property as before, and were never known to have been disturbed.

But was there not sufficient provocation for this outbreak! Was there not already cause for it in 1737, in the *infamous* "walking purchase," when the full effect of that outrageous fraud became apparent in the loss of their long-cherished possessions in the Minisink!

At the council held at Philadelphia, in 1742, called at the request of the Governor, Thomas Penn, the Delawares and Six Nations were each represented. The Governor's object was to make complaints to the latter, of the Delawares, as he had threatened in his letter of 1741, and induce the Six Nations to enforce his claim for the lands in the Minisink, as well as in the Forks, and oblige them to quit the country. There were of the Six Nations then present 230 in number. The Delawares now being under a species of vassalage to that nation.

The question of the "walking purchase," which took place in 1737, was discussed at this council.

When settlers began to move upon the lands in the Forks and the Minisink, which they did soon after this purchase was made, great dissatisfaction was expressed by the Delawares. They declared the "walk" a fraud as to the whole of the territory embraced in its limits, and particularly that portion claimed north of the Kittatinny Mountain, which included the Minisink, and they declared their determination to maintain its possession by force.

Several versions of the walk have been given, differing, however, but slightly. That rendered to Mr. John Watson by Moses Marshall, son of Edward, who had often received it from his father, is subjoined, because it is concise, and embraces, perhaps, all the facts.

"Notice was given in the public papers, that the remaining day and a half's walk was to be made, and offering 500 acres of land anywhere in the purchase, and £5 in money to the person who should attend and walk the furthest in the given time. By previous agreement the Governor was to select three white persons, and the Indians a like number of their own nation. The persons employed by the Governor were Edward Marshall, James Yates, and Solomon Jennings. One of the Indians was called Combush, but the names of the other two are forgotten.

"About the 20th of September (or when the days and nights are equal), in the year

1737, they met, before sunrise, at the old chestnut tree at Wrightstown Meeting-house, together with a great number of persons as spectators. The walkers all stood with one hand against the tree, until the sun rose, and then started.

"In two hours and a half they arrived at Red Hill in Bedminster, where Jennings and two of the Indians gave out. The other Indian (Combush) continued with them to near where the road forks at Easton, where he laid down a short time to rest; but on getting up was unable to proceed further. Marshall and Yates proceeded on, and arrived at sundown, on the north side of the Blue Mountain. They started again next morning at sunrise. While crossing a stream of water at the foot of the mountain, Yates became faint, and fell. Marshall turned back and supported him until others came to his relief, and then continued the walk alone, and arrived at noon on a spur of the Second or Broad Mountain (Pocono), estimated to be 86 miles* from the place of starting, at

* It is only about 65 miles to the Pocono, or Broad Mountain, from Wrightstown Meeting-house in a direct line.

the chestnut tree below Wrightstown Meeting-house.

"He says they walked from sunrise to sunset, without stopping, provisions and refreshments having been previously provided at different places along the road and line that had been run and marked for them to walk by to the top of the Blue Mountain; and persons also attended on horseback, by relays, with liquors of several kinds. When they arrived at the Blue Mountain they found a great number of Indians collected, expecting the walk would there end; but when they found it was to go half a day further, they were very angry, and said they were cheated—Penn had got all their good land—but that in the spring every Indian was to bring him a buckskin, and they would have their land again, and Penn might go to the devil with his poor land. An old Indian said, 'No sit down to smoke,—no shoot a squirrel; but *lun, lun, lun,* all day long!'

"Marshall says his father never received any reward for the walk, although the Governor frequently promised to have the 500 acres of land run out for him, and to which he was justly entitled."

The injustice of this walk was complained of at the time by the Indians. An ordinary day's walk was a well-defined distance by the Indians, and a day and a half's walk, as computed according to their understanding of the expression, reached from the place of starting to the south side of the Blue Mountain. But when they found Marshall's walk embraced their favorite hunting-grounds in the Minisink, and the seat of the ancient council fires of the Minsis, they were indignant beyond measure.

The Governor seems to have attached great importance to the "walking purchase," forgetting, however, that his predecessor made sale of lands in the Minisink eight or nine years before that purchase was consummated, and what was still more outrageous, if possible, the government sent up a party to survey the land and dispossess those who had previously purchased of the Indians.

This was the expedition headed by Nicholas Scull, the Surveyor General, in 1730. On this occasion they led their horses through the Water Gap, and had great difficulty in passing over the Indian trail along the river. This was just seventy years before the road through the Gap was built.

Scull and his deputy, J. Lukens, both spoke the Indian language and had employed Indian guides. They had, no doubt, as appears, "a very fatiguing journey, there being then no white inhabitants in the upper part of Bucks or Northampton counties."

The venerable Samuel Preston, from whose interesting letter, written in 1828, the above information is derived, was slightly in error in speaking of Northampton County at that date, as that stronghold of democracy was not organized into a county until twenty-two years after the event spoken of. Bucks County then extended in the Minisink, and Smithfield township had no definite limits excepting on the south, commencing at the Gap, and extending north and west as far as the white inhabitants had the temerity to penetrate in the wilderness.

When the surveying party arrived at the venerable Samuel Depui's, they found great hospitality, and plenty of the necessaries of life. The first thing that struck them with admiration was a grove of apple trees, of size far beyond any near Philadelphia.

As Samuel Depui had treated them so well, they concluded to make a survey of his *claim*, in order to befriend him, if necessary. When they began to survey, the Indians gathered round; an old Indian laid his hand on Scull's shoulder, and said, "*Put up iron string—go home.*" They quit, and returned.

This may perhaps have been one of the Indians, *Waugoanlenneggea* or *Pennoggue*, who had conveyed the same lands to Nicholas Depui three years before, in 1727, the deed for which is now in possession of the Pennsylvania Historical Society.

Mr. Depui was obliged to repurchase the land of William Allen, three years after this visit.

There is probably an error in the foregoing statement, either on the part of Mr. Preston or Nicholas Scull. The "venerable Samuel Depui" spoken of, must have been *Nicholas Depui*, the first settler. He was certainly alive when the deed from Allen was executed, in 1733. Samuel was his son.

It is perhaps unnecessary to state that long before the occurrence of the incidents here related, the "Minsis" and other tribes of the "Lenape" nation, living on or near the Delaware, were called, indiscriminately, by the white people, *Delaware Indians*, without regard to their tribal relation.

This designation commenced, of course, some years after the name of the river was changed.

Lord Delaware, in honor of whom it was renamed, came to Virginia about 1610. The Lenapes called the river *Lenape-Wihittuc*—river of the Lenapes.

For many years after the white settlers first came to the Minisink, the degradation and suffering of the Delawares, though commenced, had not penetrated this beautiful valley. They had escaped behind this mountain fastness, the devastating storm that was raging without, and their scattered numbers who felt its withering blast came here for a refuge, and to cluster round the seat of their ancient council fires, to chant anthems of the glorious past and to weep over the ruin that was portending.

They felt that they had one spot left, and one very dear, that they could yet claim as their own, and call by the fond name of home.

Alas! how few the years before the compass and "iron string" encircled the last forest and blasted the last hope of the greatest of the Lenapes on the banks of Lenape's river.

The continued peace and security which the early settlers enjoyed in this valley, and particularly at this juncture, when the Indians were suffering so much on every hand by the intrigues of the whites and the cruelty of their enemies, is proof of the amiable character of the Minsi Indians, and that they were at all times inclined to deal justly and live fraternally with those who manifested a like disposition.

What remains to be said of these people, or all that can be said in this connection, is but little, and that little very sad.

Teedyuscung had since the cruel decree of 1742, been collecting the scattered remnants of the Delawares together for their final exit. No rest for the soles of their feet in all this broad domain. Scarce a hiding-place for the hunted fugitives, whose nation once ruled an empire of such grand proportions. They fled to Wyoming, where, in 1763, their chief was burned to death in his own wigwam, by some emissary of the Six Nations.

A Christian of their tribe named *Netawatawees*, was chosen chief. They moved to Wyalusing, formed a colony, commenced the cultivation of the soil, built a church and comfortable dwellings, and were pursuing the lives of civilized men. They prospered greatly, and all things seemed for a time encouraging.

But the inevitable "John Smith," in the form of a land speculator, was on their track. A warrant was laid upon the lands they had chosen, and the government sustained the claim. The "iron string" again encircled their home; their houses and church as well as their lands became the property of others.

And now, fugitives again, we hear of them next on the Muskingum, their chief dead from grief, and *Coquehageton* his successor. They are now in the midst of the Revolution. The Six Nations as well as some of their own scattered numbers have joined the British forces. What will this remnant of the Delawares do? They dare not remain neutral, and what hope have they in the success of either of the contending parties! General Brodhead has command at Fort Pitt. He sends for the chief Coquehageton. He states the perilous situation of his army, and sues for the aid of the Delawares.

The chief of a ruined nation, not in anger but in sorrow, relates their grievances and the sufferings his people have endured by those who now call upon them for assistance. Moved to tears by the recital of his own sad history, he ends by teaching us

> "How beautifully falls from human lips,
> The blessed word forgive."

He joins the American standard. The war-cry is once more heard among those who were so recently taught by Christian men the lessons of peace; but this time they are to engage in a cause from which they have all to lose and nothing to gain.

> "Mad from life's history,
> Glad of death's mystery,
> Swift to be hurled—
> Anywhere, anywhere,
> Out of the world."

*Early Settlements in the Minisink.**

It is difficult to determine the exact date of the first European settlement in the upper valley of the Delaware. That there were white people here at an early period, even before the arrival of William Penn at Philadelphia, seems now to be generally admitted; but it must be confessed that concerning those who inhabited the Minisink previous to 1725, we have very little knowledge.

The Depuis and Van Campens, were the first settlers in the lower Minisink whose family we are enabled to trace.

It is quite certain that the first tide of immigration into this valley, flowed from the direction of the Hudson, and so down the valleys of the Mamakating and Naversink, and entering the Minisink at the Dela-

* The History of the Minisink, now in course of preparation, and from which a few extracts are here given, will embrace some account of each of the early families settled in the neighborhood, and the author will be glad to receive from any member of such families, whatever information of general interest he may possess—the date of their arrival in the country, the names of each of the descendants still residing here, &c.

ware, spread throughout its borders. Previous to 1780 there were very few settlers here from any other direction. They made selection of the level lands along the river, and in a few instances their descendants occupy the original possession.

A receding wave as it may be termed, set in from the southwest after 1780, bringing mainly descendants from the early settlers in Philadelphia, Bucks, and Northampton Counties. This class, located in Cherry Valley, on Brodhead's Creek, and the Valley of the Pocono. This immigration continued till about the year 1800.

A second wave flowing from the same direction, brought to Stroudsburg and vicinity, a considerable class of our most respectable citizens, mostly from Bucks County. In the same tide came the Germans from what is known as the "Dry Lands," of Northampton County. They swept by the valley settlers and located on the higher lands overlooking the river. The whole range of what is known as the Shawnee Hills, extending from Brodhead's Creek to the Delaware, below the mouth of the Bushkill, is almost entirely owned and occupied by this class of people.

This immigration took place between the years 1800 and 1820.

Among the first settlers of the Minisink, up to 1780, many of whose decendants still reside here, we find the names of Depui, Van Campen, Van Auken, Van Etten, Van Demark, Westbrook, Westfall, Brink, Shoemaker, Chambers, De Witt, Brodhead, Hyndshaw, McMichael, McDowell, Drake, Stroud, Rosenkrance, Quick, Jayne, Fish, Price, Cortright, Transue, Storm, Middaugh, Dingman, La Bar, Hanna, Decker, Bossard, Bittenbender, Wills, Detrick, Keller, Smith, Long, Miller, Logan, Hauser, Bush, Hilborn, Benson, Van Vliet, Learn, Shaw, Overfield, Coolbaugh, Peters, Brown, Kuykendall, &c.

The first families, settled in the *lower portion* of the Minisink, of whom we can now give a connected genealogy, are the Depuis, Van Campens, Brodheads, and Strouds.

Depui Family.

Nicholas Depui was a Huguenot—French Protestant of the period of the religious wars in that country—who, with many others, fled from France to Holland in the year 1685, when Louis XIV exposed them to Papal vengeance by revoking the edict of Nantes.

It was, probably, soon after this date that Mr. Depui, having fled to Holland, came with others from that country, and settled in New York.

He lived a short time at Esopus, and came to the Minisink in 1725.

He purchased a large portion of the level land in which the present town of Shawnee is situated, of the Minsi Indians, in 1727, and likewise the two large Islands in the Delaware—Shawano and Manwalamink. He also purchased the same property of William Allen in 1733.

Few communities can lay claim to a family of greater worth and respectability; and fewer still can witness a reputation, such as this family possessed, maintained untarnished for five successive generations.

For nearly half a century, Mr. Depui and other members of his family continued in undisturbed friendship with the Indians of the Minisink; and after the main body of the tribe were exiled, the few who fondly lingered until the outbreak of 1755—when they were hunted like wild beasts of the forest—ever found a generous welcome at his door.

Mr. Robert Reading Depui, of Stroudsburg, is the sole surviving representative of this branch of the family in the Minisink. He still owns the large stone mansion, located on the original purchase, and also the upper island, known in the earlier records as "Manwalamink."

His father was named Nicholas; his grandfather, Nicholas; his great-grandfather, Samuel; his great-great-grandfather, Nicholas.

A more complete genealogy will be given, in the work contemplated, of this and other families in the Minisink, and also their connection with the history of the Valley.

There was another family of Depuis, probably relatives of the first Nicholas, in the Minisink, residing first in New Jersey, near Flat Brook.

Daniel, Benjamin, Aaron, and John, are mentioned at an early period. The venerable Aaron Depui, who died a few years ago, was a descendant of one of these, and whose children, grandchildren, and great-grandchildren number many hundreds at this time. Daniel Depui purchased the grist mill and 54 acres of land of Nicholas Depui in 1753. Aaron Depui, with Charles Brodhead and Benjamin Shoemaker, were commissioned by Governor Morris to treat with the Susquehanna Indians in 1755. Soon after, Aaron Depui had charge of a company to go to the Susquehanna, but was detained in order to give protection to the settlers in the Minisink, who were invaded by the Indians.

There was also a Moses Depui here, who was appointed a magistrate in 1747.

Van Campen Family.

Col. Abram Van Campen came to the Minisink about the same time as Mr. Depui. He purchased a large body of land in what is now called Pahaquarra (Pahaqualine), on the opposite side of the river, five miles above Nicholas Depuis.

Abram Van Campen had four sons, Benjamin, Moses, Abram, and John. Benjamin died young.

Abram had two sons, named James and Abram.

John had one son, named Abram.

Abram* the son of Abram, and grandson of Abram, had one son, who is the venerable Moses Van Campen, now living on a part of the original purchase of his great-grandfather.

The Van Campens were always an influential and highly respectable family in the Minisink. Col. Abram Van Campen was prominent in the early history of this portion of New Jersey. He was actively engaged in defending the frontier, during the Indian war of 1755, and was one of the first judges of the county of Sussex, in New Jersey (which then embraced a portion of the Minisink), which was organized on the 20th November, 1753. Jonathan Robeson,† Abram

* John Adams, while attending Congress, during its sessions at Philadelphia, as late as 1800, passed down the "Mine road" as the most eligible route from Boston to that city. He was accustomed to lodge at Squire Van Campen's, in the Jersey Minisinks.—*Information from Albert G. Brodhead, Esq., of Bethlehem—Reichel's Memorials of the Moravian Church.*

† Jonathan Robeson was the grandson of Andrew Robeson, who came to America with William Penn, and was a

Van Campen, John Anderson, Jonathan Petitt, and Thomas Wolverton, Esqs., were, by the order of his Majesty, King George II, commissioned Judges of the Pleas, with power likewise to act as Justices of the Peace.

John Van Campen, son of Col. Abram, actively espoused the cause of the Pennamites in the Connecticut troubles, and was in frequent correspondence with President Reed during the Revolution. He lived in the stone house which stood in Shawnee, where the residence of Mr. George V. Bush is now located; the latter, with Benjamin V. Bush, Esq., are his grandsons.

Brodhead Family.

Daniel Brodhead was the ancestor of those who bear the name in the United States. He was born in Yorkshire, England, and

member of Governor Markham's Privy Council. The present Secretary of the Navy is a descendant in the seventh generation. The Secretary's father, grandfather, great-grandfather, great-great-grandfather, great-great-great-grandfather, and great-great-great-great-grandfather each in his turn have worn the judicial ermine.

was a captain of grenadiers, and a royalist in the reign of King Charles II, by whom he was ordered to join the expedition under Col. Nichols, which captured New Netherlands (New York) from the Dutch in 1664. He settled in Ulster County, N. Y., was commander-in-chief of the militia forces at Kingston in 1665, and died in 1670. By his wife Ann Tye, he had three sons, *Daniel*, *Charles*, and *Richard*.

SECOND GENERATION.

1. Daniel, died young.

2. Charles, married Maria Tenbrook, of Ulster County, and had four children, one of whom was named *Wessel*.

3. Richard, was born in 1666, in Marbletown; married Miss Jansen, by whom he had one son, named Daniel.

THIRD GENERATION.

1. Wessel Brodhead, son of Charles, was the father of the Rev. Jacob Brodhead, who preached many years ago in the Dutch Re-

formed Church in Crown Street, Philadelphia, and afterwards in Brooklyn, at which city he died. Jacob Brodhead was the father of John Romeyn Brodhead the historian, now living in New York.

2. Daniel Brodhead, son of Richard, was born at Marbletown, N. Y., in 1693; he married Hester Wyngart, and moved to Pennsylvania in 1737. He settled on Analoming Creek, called since that time Brodhead's Creek. He purchased 640 acres of land, in the centre of which East Stroudsburg is now located. The western boundary line started near the old forge, passed near the graveyard, and continued on the west side of the creek till beyond what is called the "Flower Garden." Besides East Stroudsburg, the tract embraced the properties now owned by Mr. Robert Brown and Mr. Christian Smith. He afterwards purchased what is now the eastern portion of Stroudsburg, as far as the mill-dam of Mr. William Wallace. He called the settlement Dansbury, and it was known by that name till Stroudsburg was founded by Jacob Stroud in 1769.

In 1744 Daniel Brodhead first became acquainted with the Moravian Missionaries,

Shaw, *Bruce*, and *Mack*, whose way to Shekomeko (in Dutchess Co., N. Y.), passed through his settlement. With the character of these self-sacrificing Christian men he was very favorably impressed, and was their warm friend and supporter ever after, in the face of much *influential opposition* at the time. They established a mission-house on his property, which was situated on the west side of the creek, near the iron bridge, and was called Dansbury mission. In the outbreak of 1755, he is represented as a man of great courage and intrepidity, remaining with his sons and defending his family, and others who came there for assistance, against the attacks of the Indians, when the whole surrounding country had been abandoned.

Daniel Brodhead had ten children. Four sons and one daughter survived him, named, Daniel, Garret, Charles, Luke, and Ann Garten.

He died on a visit to Bethlehem, July 22d, 1755.

Fourth Generation.

Sons of Daniel:

1. Daniel, married Elizabeth Depui, daughter of Samuel Depui, of Smithfield. After her death, he married Gov. Mifflin's widow. He left several daughters, and one son, named Daniel, who died when a young man.

He was a general in the army of the Revolution, and had command at Fort Pitt, in 1780, and after the war, was appointed Surveyor-General.

2. Garret Brodhead was also an officer of the Revolutionary army. Richard Brodhead and John Brodhead were his sons.

Albert Gallatin Brodhead, of Bethlehem, William Brodhead and Garret Brodhead, of Pike County, Charles Brodhead, who died several years ago, and the late Hon. Richard Brodhead, U. S. Senator, are sons of Richard. The sons of John were Daniel Mifflin Brodhead, John Hena Brodhead, Henry Brodhead, and William Franklin Brodhead. John H. is the only one living of the sons of John.

Charles Brodhead, of Bethlehem, is a son of Albert Gallatin; Frank Brodhead, of Port

Jervis, is a son of William; Albert G. Brodhead, Jr., of Mauch Chunk, is a son of Garret; Charles D. Brodhead, of Stroudsburg, is a son of Charles; John Brodhead, formerly of Philadelphia, and President of the Camden and Atlantic City Railroad, is a son of Daniel Mifflin; Rev. Augustus Brodhead, missionary to India, is a son of John H.; Richard Brodhead, at Bethlehem, is a son of the late Hon. Richard.

3. Charles Brodhead was appointed one of the first magistrates in the Minisink.* He was also appointed by Gov. Morris to treat with the Indians on the Susquehanna, in 1755, and gave great offence to the chief of the Delawares, Teedyuscung, by reporting him to the governor as secretly unfriendly to the English. He married, and moved to the State of New York. He was the father of the Hon. John C. Brodhead, and Daniel Brodhead, M. C. from that State.

* The first commissions appear to have been made out to Charles Brodhead and Moses Depui in 1747. But Nicholas Depui certainly seems to have acted in the capacity of an officer of that kind several years before. "In 1740 Nicholas Depui, of Smithfield, in the Minisink, gave an order on the treasurer of Bucks County, for the payment of bounty on sixteen wolf scalps, delivered to him and killed by one man."

4. Luke Brodhead was a captain during a greater part of the Revolution, and was commissioned a colonel the same day as his brother, the general. He was an intimate friend of Lafayette, and was desperately wounded at the battle of Brandywine.

He was appointed magistrate during the Connecticut troubles in Wyoming, though still residing in Smithfield. He married Elizabeth Harrison, and had five sons and three daughters: Thomas, John, Luke, Daniel, Alexander, Elizabeth, Ann, and Rachel. He died in Smithfield, in 1805.

Fifth Generation.

Sons of Luke:

1. Thomas Brodhead went from Smithfield to the State of New York when young; married Miss Livingston, of "Livingston's Manor." He was a physician of great eminence, and died about 1830. Col. Thomas Brodhead Van Buren is his grandson.

2. John Brodhead left Smithfield for New Hampshire at 18 years of age; was a Methodist clergyman and Presiding Elder; was also

member of the Legislature of that State, and was for several years member of Congress. He married Mary Dodge, and had six sons and three daughters: Col. Daniel Dodge, of Boston, late Navy Agent; John Montgomery, Second Comptroller, Washington; Joseph Crawford (died recently); George Hamilton, Secretary Board of Brokers, New York; Thornton Fleming, Colonel of the Third Michigan Cavalry Regiment, was killed in the second Bull Run engagement; and Josiah Adams, of Boston. Rev. John Brodhead died April 7th, 1838.

3. Luke Brodhead married Elizabeth Wills, granddaughter of Col. William Wills. They had eight sons and one daughter. Of the excellence of his own parents it does not become the writer to speak. His father died in Smithfield, March 21st, 1845. His venerated mother is still living.

4. Daniel Brodhead moved to Owasco, N. Y., and married Miss Hardenburg. He had three sons and three daughters: Jacob, Luke, and Dr. John Alexander.

5. Alexander Brodhead moved to Hunterdon County, N. J., and married Miss Bloom. He had three sons and three daughters, John, Jacob, and Herbert.

Sixth Generation.

Daughter and sons of Luke and Elizabeth Brodhead: Elizabeth, William Alexander, Thomas, Theodore, Lewis, Luke Wills, Horace Binney, De Witt Clinton, and Benjamin Franklin.

Seventh Generation.

1. Mary A. and William Augustus, daughter and son of Elizabeth and Thomas J. Albright.
2. Edward Livingston and John Davis, sons of William A. and Mary Brodhead.
3. Eugene, son of Thomas and Hannah M. Brodhead.
4. Harry Wills, son of Theodore and Emma H. Brodhead.
5. Cicero, son of Luke Wills and Leonora S. Brodhead.
6. Bella, daughter of Benjamin F. and Emily K. Brodhead.

Eighth Generation.

To this generation belong the children of Charles Brodhead, of Bethlehem, and those of his cousins named as descendants of Garret, of the fourth generation; William Hollinshead, of Stroudsburg, is also of this generation, and the children of Dr. H. R. Linderman, Dr. G. B. Linderman, and the Hon. M. M. Dimmick, of Mauch Chunk; Edward Pinchot, and J. Wallace, of Milford, and Jesse R. Smith, who owns and resides upon a portion of the original purchase made by his great-great-great-great-great-grandfather, in 1737.

Ninth Generation.

Of this generation are the children of Dr. A. R. Jackson, Mrs. Jane Hollinshead, and the grandchildren of Hon. M. M. Dimmick.

The writer hopes to escape the charge of partiality, in giving so extended an account of the Brodhead family. It is only done because he happens to know most of that family. He will be only too glad to be able to give as full an account of each of the old families in the Minisink.

Stroud Family.

Jacob Stroud was born at Amwell, N. J., in 1735. He, with three brothers, entered the provincial army, and participated in the engagement at "Fort William Henry" and at the "Plains of Abraham," at the taking of Quebec, where the commanders of both the English and French armies, General Wolf and General Montcalm, lost their lives.

Jacob Stroud, John Fish,* and Mathias Hutchinson,† were the three persons nearest General Wolf when he fell, and carried him behind the rocks before he expired.

One of the Stroud brothers lost his life in this engagement.

Soon after the close of the French and Indian war, Jacob Stroud came to this valley,

* John Fish was the father of Ashbel Fish and grandfather of *fighting Abner*, who lived near Stroudsburg a few years ago.

Hon. Paul S. Preston, from whom this information is derived, calls them "a giant race of men."

† Mathias Hutchinson was an Associate Judge in Bucks County, previous to the Revolution.

then a young man about 28 years of age. He purchased the property on McMichael's Creek, now owned by John W. Huston, of John McMichael, in 1769. This property is about two miles west of where he afterwards located the town of Stroudsburg.

The first buildings erected at the latter place, were the large stone mansion now the residence of his grandson James H. Stroud; the frame dwelling which stood in the centre of the town, opposite the Stroudsburg House, and the Fort Penn mansion on the site of the old fort of that name, which formed a part of the block damaged by the late freshet. Fort Penn was erected during the Revolution, and Fort Hamilton in 1756; the latter stood near the dwelling of the late Samuel Stokes. Jacob Stroud was a colonel in the Revolutionary Army, and had command here of Fort Penn. He was a member of the Convention which formed the *first* Constitution of Pennsylvania, A. D. 1776.

He married a sister of John McDowell, whose father came to the Minisink in company with Nicholas Depui in 1725, and purchased the property in Cherry Valley, now known as Shaw's Meadows, in 1748.

Jacob Stroud raised a large, influential, and highly respectable family, some of the descendants of whom now hold honorable positions in the country.

The children of Jacob Stroud were: Hannah, who married John Starbird; John, who married Elizabeth Depui; Jane, who married John Bush; Sarah, who married James Hollinshead; Daniel, who married Elizabeth Shoemaker; Rachel, who married Samuel Rees; Ann, who married Peter Hollinshead; Deborah, who married James Burson; Elizabeth, who married William Colbert; Jemima, who married Edward Burson; and Jacob, who died young.

Colonel Jacob Stroud died in 1806, and was then the owner of 4000 acres of land in this neighborhood.

Daniel Stroud, son of Colonel Stroud, was, during his life, one of the most intelligent and influential men of this community.

He laid out the town on its present liberal plan of broad avenues, and, in addition, enjoined in his deed of sale to all purchasers, that they should set their houses thirty feet back from the sidewalk. This gives to the residences of this beautiful town, that quiet rural air so much admired in New England villages.

The memory of Daniel Stroud is cherished by many now living in this community.

The Hon. George M. Stroud, of Philadelphia, and James H. Stroud, Esq., of Stroudsburg, are the surviving sons of Daniel. There is a large family connection, which we hope to trace hereafter.

There are many interesting incidents in the life of Hannah, who married John Starbird. She was on many accounts a most remarkable woman.

Her memory was so retentive that she could name the birthday of all the young people of her acquaintance, when their parents were married, to whom they were related, where they were from, and when the family came in the country, &c. Great events, as well as the minor incidents of domestic life, were equally well remembered. When an aged lady she could tell the number of pounds of butter sold from her dairy at each year, for the long period her husband had been engaged in farming, the price at which it was sold and the name of each individual purchaser, and so with regard to all the other products of the farm.

Before her marriage she assisted her father in the store, and frequently did the buying of the goods as well as the selling. For this purpose she would ride to Philadelphia on horseback unattended. At that early period, between 1780 and 1790, much of the country, especially between Stroudsburg and Easton, was an almost unbroken wilderness. The Revolution for the first part of the time was not yet ended, and prowling bands of Indians not unfrequent. The roads were rough, the streams unbridged, the forests long and gloomy, and the places of entertainment few and far between.

Early Settlements at the Delaware Water Gap.

Long after the settlements made north of the mountain, the Water Gap remained a solitary wilderness, and the wild beasts, common to the primitive forest, resorted hither as a place of security after their other haunts had been invaded by the early pioneers.* The Gap offered no inducement to the tillers of the soil, and the dark gloomy gorge, then overshadowed with the forest oaks and pines of the growth of centuries, was too forbidding in its aspect for the abode of any but those who wished to avoid contact with civilized men. The story is told of a solitary individual inhabiting a hut in summer, near the Indian Ladder, in which he coined money from metals procured in some cavern in the mountain, and in winter lived in a palatial residence with his family in a remote city.

An Indian trail wound along the base of the mountain through the gorge on either side of the river, and an occasional equestrian managed to lead his horse over the Indian path.

In the year 1730, the government of the province of Pennsylvania sent up agents to the Minisink, to dispossess certain persons of lands, held by purchase of the Indians. This party, it is said, managed with great

* An old and respectable citizen of the neighborhood remembers, when a boy, to have seen a herd of deer, five in number, feeding in what is now the lawn in front of the Kittatinny House.

difficulty to lead their horses through the Gap. At a later period, in 1743, as has been stated elsewhere, the Rev. David Brainerd, in a missionary tour amongst the Indians in the Minisink, did not, it appears, consider the passage practicable.

It was not until the year 1800, that the construction of a wagon-road was undertaken, and then by individual subscriptions on the part of those residing above and below the mountain.

About this time, a small log house was erected by some daring adventurer, within a few feet of where the Kittatinny House now stands. For a time,—about the year 1808, and for some years after,—there lived in this house of two rooms and an attic, a tall, white-haired, dignified-looking man, with wife and daughter of corresponding gentility. The interior of the rude dwelling had an air of refinement, and its inmates bore evidence of having seen more prosperous days. The costly furniture, gilded mirrors, and a well-stocked library, contrasted strangely with the simple abode and its wild surroundings; and marvellous, indeed, were the tales passing current for a time with the rustic youth of the neighborhood of the wonderful wealth and mysterious doings of its isolated inhabitants. The master occupant of this establishment was none other than the notorious Alexander Patterson.

In the year 1793, there came to the Water Gap from St. Domingo a Frenchman named Anthony Dutot, having left there hastily with others, at the time when the order of possession on that island was reversed, when the servants became the masters of the soil, and the masters became fugitives. He was said to be wealthy, and buried on his plantation a considerable amount of gold and silver, and brought with him what coin he could conveniently transport. Mr. Dutot was a man of some degree of culture and refinement, and after spending a short time in Philadelphia, he proceeded up the Delaware in search of a future home. He was impressed with the grandeur of the scenery at the Delaware Water Gap, and eagerly made purchase of a large tract of land, previously considered as worthless, including the portion on which the Kittatinny House is situated, and the hills on the north side of the mountain where the village is located. At the latter place he laid out a city and called it after his own name, and, like the founder of the Roman commonwealth, chose for its location the hills overlooking the plain. In the centre of the plot, around which he built a dozen or more small dwellings, he left a large triangular lot for a market-place. The "city" has never grown, however, to the proportions of more than a hamlet. The name has been changed to *Delaware Water Gap*, and the buildings erected by Mr. Dutot have long since disappeared, and others more substantial have taken their place; but the market-grounds still remain uninvaded.

The first wagon-road through the Gap passed round the east end of the inclosure in front of the Kittatinny House, and over Sunset Hill, intersecting the present road near the Church of the Mountain. Soon after the building of this road, Mr. Dutot obtained a charter for a *toll-road*, extending from the foot of the hill along the bank of the river, where the railroad now passes, to the village. He lived at this time in a house which stood near the old saw-mill, and there the "gate" was located. The toll-road was never profitable, and caused him much annoyance. Various devices were resorted to, on the part of travellers, to avoid payment, sometimes by driving rapidly through the gateway, and at others by pretending not to understand his meaning. Mr. Dutot never learned to speak the English language correctly, and his courteous demand for "*von leetle toll*," accompanied with a polite bow, was pretended to be understood for the usual salutation at parting, and a polite "good day, sir," with an equally profound bow on the part of the delinquent traveller, was usually the only compensation received, until he was obliged, at length, to resort to harsher measures. The toll-road was superseded in 1823 by the construction of the present state road, along the southeastern slope of Sunset Hill.

Mr. Dutot built the saw-mill upon the foundation now to be seen at the boat-landing, and it was continued in use till burned by sparks from a locomotive soon after the opening of the railroad.

In the year 1829, he commenced the erection of a small portion of what is now the

Kittatinny House, but unfortunately failed in business before its completion.

He had made an injudicious use of his funds, and among other non-paying enterprises, spent large sums of money in making excavations in the mountain in search of minerals. He had also a number of expensive lawsuits with his neighbor, Ulrick Hauser.

Mr. Hauser resided on the property now known as the "River Farm," owned by Mr. Evan T. Croasdale. He was a German, and came to the country a few years previous to the arrival of Mr. Dutot.

It is said they seldom met without disputing, but how they managed to quarrel, when neither understood the other's language, is not easily explained. That there was a *misunderstanding* is quite evident, and that unfortunate condition of things seems to have continued after both began to be understood in the same dialect, for we find in later years that Mr. Dutot was indicted by the grand jury at Easton for an assault and battery on the person of Mr. Hauser.

The version given of the affair by Mr. Dutot before the court, as far as remembered, is as follows: "Mr. Hause, he von grand what you call him—he no tell ze true; he call my little ceete *Hard Scrab* (Hard Scrabble); then I say, 'Zounds, Mr. Hause, you be von Hard Scrab yourself;' then Mr. Hause, he put his fist in his hand and strike me; then I lift my foot and I strike Mr. Hause."

Soon after Mr. Dutot's settlement here, he made selection of Sunset Hill as his last resting-place, and some twenty years before his death, purchased a bell and cannon, the former to be rung from the belfry of his own house, on which it was erected, and the latter to be fired from his grave when certain events transpired, affecting the prosperity of the place, which he predicted would occur. Among the incidents remembered were the completion of a railroad through the Gap, and the landing of a steamboat at the wharf he had made selection of on the bank of the Delaware. He died in 1841, and fifteen years after, the whistle of the locomotive was first heard echoing in the gorge of the mountain, but the old gentleman's repose was undisturbed by the ringing of bell or the firing of cannon over his solitary and neglected grave.

The cannon long since exploded in saluting the dawn of a national anniversary from the summit of Mount Caroline. But the old bell is this morning pealing, in unaltered tone, from the belfry of the old stone seminary at Stroudsburg, summoning the reluctant girls and boys of a third generation.

First Visitors.

The first visitors at the Delaware Gap remembered were from Philadelphia, and about the year 1820. At that time there was no building on the present site, excepting the hut heretofore alluded to.

Primitive forest trees then studded the lawn, and an occasional traveller, who wished to evade the payment of toll on Mr. Dutot's better road along the river-bank, passed by Mr. Patterson's solitary abode.

These first visitors sojourned at the home of the writer's father in the village, and the names of Horace Binney and Caleb Cope are among those remembered by his mother.

In 1832, Samuel Snyder purchased the property, with the view of making it a place of resort; and to his memory the credit is due of bringing it into public notice, and for giving the Kittatinny House a character for neatness, cleanliness, and comfort, that has required much effort on the part of his successors to maintain. Mr. Snyder moved here in the spring of 1833, and enlarged and completed the building commenced by Mr. Dutot. The house then accommodated about twenty-five persons, and was filled the same summer, and before it was fairly furnished. Among the first guests were Mrs. Swift, Miss Coffman, Caleb Cope and family, and General Cadwalader.

William A. Brodhead rented the Kittatinny House, and moved here in 1841. In 1851, he purchased, and increased its capacity to accommodate sixty persons. In 1853, it was again increased to seventy-five. In 1860, to one hundred and fifty. In 1862, to one hundred and seventy-five; and in 1866, to two hundred and fifty.

Durham Boats.

Long before any facilities, other than the rough wagon-roads of the times, were afforded the people, both north and south of the mountain, for the transportation of the products of the Valley of the Delaware to market, the old Furnace at Durham, on the Delaware, a few miles below Easton, had constructed, about the year 1750, a class of boats, somewhat longer and narrower than the present canal-boats, and in shape resembling a weaver's shuttle. The deck extended a few feet only from stem and stern. The "captain," or steersman, stood on the stern-deck, and guided the boat with a long rudder. A narrow planking on either side afforded the walking-place for the pikemen, who with long poles or pikes propelled the boat up the current.

These were called Durham boats, and soon came into general use on the Delaware.

They were used as early as 1758, by John Van Campen, for the transportation of flour to Philadelphia, manufactured from wheat grown in the Minisink. Mr. Van Campen's mill was at Shawnee, and stood near where Mr. Wilson's mill is now located.

"In 1786, one Jesse Dickinson came from Philadelphia, and laid out a city in Delaware County, New York, called 'Dickinson City.' It was situated near what is now called Cannonsville. Mr. Dickinson brought his men and building materials up the Delaware in Durham boats."*

The old firm of Bell & Thomas at Experiment Mills, known for their energy and integrity, and pleasantly remembered by many still living, used the Durham boats extensively in their day, both in the transportation of flour to Philadelphia, and in bringing up supplies for the neighborhood.

The semi-monthly arrival of these boats at "Armat's Landing," in those days, was an event of much greater interest to the people of the neighborhood than the landing of a steamer from Europe is to the citizens of Philadelphia, at the present day.

The boatmen were a strong, hardy set of men, and seemed to enjoy their laborious occupation. The "captain," feeling the re-

* Gould's History of Delaware County.

sponsibility of his position, bore himself with great dignity, especially on his arrival at "port;" and the boys who collected about the wharf when the vessel hove in sight, were terror-stricken at the imperious manner of the captain, and the stentorian tones by which he commanded all alike, on board and on shore.

After the completion of the Delaware division of the Pennsylvania Canal, the Durham boats began gradually to disappear, so that now one is seldom seen on the waters of the Delaware.

Steamboat "Alfred Thomas."

Mr. Dutot's prediction in reference to steamboat navigation on the upper waters of the Delaware is not yet verified.

The attempt, however, has been made, and but for the unfortunate occurrence attending the first effort, we should now have the pleasure of one of the finest excursions to be enjoyed on any river in the States, between Belvidere and Port Jervis.

An act of incorporation was granted in

1860 to the "Kittatinny Improvement Company," with power to improve the navigation of the Delaware River, and "to run one or more boats propelled by steam or caloric engines, or otherwise, with such appurtenances and equipments as may be deemed adequate, &c., between the head of Foul Rift and the village of Matamoras."

After considerable money was expended on the most difficult portions of the river, an experienced committee was appointed, who, after examination, pronounced the navigation between the points named, entirely practicable.

A steamboat was accordingly built at Easton in the winter and spring of 1860, called the "Alfred Thomas," of the following dimensions: fourteen feet in width, eighty-five feet in length, and of one hundred tons burden, and on the 6th of March of that year, was ready for the previously-arranged excursion.

"On the morning of the 6th of March, 1860, with a beautiful Union flag flying from her upper deck, and with about one hundred persons on board, including the proprietors, and a number of other gentlemen from Belvidere, she steamed off from the boat-yard, where she had lain so long, and passed down the Lehigh to the bosom of the Delaware, where she was destined. Crowds of people lined the shores of the river, watching her appearance, and a beautiful sight was presented as the gallant little boat ploughed her way up the stream, while crowds on the shore, as well as those on board, cheered heartily.

"At the bridge, which she reached at noon, the steamer stopped, when all but about thirty on board got off, the remainder intending to go to Belvidere, where the boat was expected shortly to arrive, and where numbers of citizens were waiting with joyful anticipations. . . .

"The day was, indeed, a most beautiful one, and the navigation of the upper Delaware by steam seemed truly to have an auspicious beginning; but, one short hour sufficed to bring about the sad change. The engineer ran the pressure of steam up to one hundred and twenty-five pounds to the square inch, when it should not have exceeded eighty,—the consequence of which was the explosion of the boiler, and the most appalling calamity that has ever occurred in this place was witnessed."*

Thirteen of the number on board were killed, or died soon after, and several were more or less seriously injured. Among the former were Judge William R. Sharp and Richard Holcomb, who, with Alfred Thomas, were the original projectors of the enterprise.

First Telegraphic Message to the Delaware Water Gap.

MESSAGE NO. 1.

EASTON, July 11th, 1855, 9 o'clock A. M.

"To the ladies and gentlemen now at the Kittatinny House:

"The Easton office takes pleasure in being the medium of congratulation to you on the part of the citizens of Easton upon the completion of the lightning line to the 'Gap.' We are no longer separated by time or space; and we heartily and most cordially salute your introduction into the great mag-

* Reporter of the *Easton Daily Express.*

netic circle, which now includes almost the entire civilized world. Our compliments to the *beauty* and *manly gallantry* of the picturesque *Gap*."

"J. L. MINGLE."

Railroads.

The Delaware Water Gap is reached from Philadelphia by the Philadelphia and Trenton Railroad, and Belvidere, Delaware, and Flemington Railroad to *Manunka Chunk*,* and from thence by the Delaware, Lackawanna, and Western Railroad. From New York by the "Central, of New Jersey," to *New Hampton*, and thence by the *Warren* and the Delaware, Lackawanna, and Western. The last-named road passes through the gorge of the mountain and along the bank of the river at the base of the cliff on which the Hotel is situated. It runs at nearly right angles with the Delaware soon after leaving the station at this place, and follows

* The Indian name of the range of hills terminating at the station was Penungauchung, and it is to be regretted that it was not preserved in naming this station.

up the windings of Brodhead's Creek, some ten miles, thence through a wild, picturesque country, for nearly the whole distance, to Scranton. When on the summit of the Pocono Mountain, which is gained by a rapidly ascending grade from the river, a view is afforded of great extent, variety, and beauty, and is worth a journey over the road to witness.

A wilderness of vast extent, covering thousands of acres between the Pocono and Blue Ridge, lies before you; and, deep below you, a valley of hills, a grand foreground to the wonderful, inimitable picture Nature has wrought, with the deep mountain gorge in distant perspective.

This view is obtained immediately after you pass through the tunnel on the point of the mountain, and by an intimation to either of the gentlemanly conductors on this road, you will be afforded facilities for witnessing it, that, perhaps, would not otherwise be obtained.

The Delaware, Lackawanna, and Western Railroad was completed in 1855, at a cost, including equipments, of over 12,000,000 dollars. The total length from Great Bend to the Delaware River is one hundred and thirteen miles. It was a work of great magnitude, and is a monument to the enterprise and perseverance of its original projectors.

The Belvidere, Delaware and Flemington Railroad passes for the whole distance, from Trenton to Manunka Chunk, along the bank of the Delaware River, "and one's eyes seldom look upon a more enchanting series of landscapes than stretches along this river, in one long and varied line of beauty, from New Hope and the Nockamixon Rocks to the Delaware Water Gap."

This road possesses the reputation of admirable management, of which its cleanly and comfortable passenger cars give good evidence.

Extract from a Letter of M. R. Hulce, Esq.

My dear Sir: Lake "Utsayantha" is near the head of the main or Mohawk branch of the Delaware River (sometimes called the west branch), and is situated partly in Delaware and partly in Schoharie Counties, the line of the counties running through it. Its outlet is in the town of Harpersfield, and in a map of 1779 is named *Ustayantha.* The lake is clear as crystal and circular in form, and contains, I should judge, about 60 or 70 acres. It is above tide-water, 1888 feet.

The Cochecton Valley was first settled by white men from Connecticut, in 1757. In 1762, there were thirty houses, one sawmill, one grist mill, and a blockhouse, or wooden fort. Daniel Skinner ran the first raft from Cochecton, soon after the close of the old French War, or between 1760 and 1770, with Josiah Parks as fore-hand.

The Delaware rises on the western slope of the Catskill. Mount Prospect, a mile or two southeast of its source, rises about 1500 feet higher, and from its summit, Albany, some 70 miles distant, can be plainly seen on a clear day. Your beautiful and picturesque home and delightful summer resort is nestled in one of the gorges of the oldest of earth's upheavals. Long before the snow-clad Alps or the Rocky Mountains emerged from their ocean beds, and before the carboniferous period, the crests of the Kittatinny pierced the clouds, while their sides were laved by the vast expanse of waters whence they had risen when "the mountains were brought forth."

The grand scenery of our noble Delaware, for the first two hundred miles, as it hugs the north-western slopes of this Titanic range, seeking an outlet, well repays a visit on a raft. It is evident that for ages a barrier existed at your place, which dammed back the river, perhaps one hundred miles. Whether the "Gap" was made by the slow action of the waters over a fall like Niagara, or by some earthquake convulsion, it is difficult to determine. The draining of the waters left the valley of the Minisink, as it now exists, a rich garden. This valley was settled by the Dutch, about one hundred years before Penn founded Philadelphia. A road was built from "Sopies" (now Kingston) into the valley, the remains of which are still to be seen. It was called "The Mine Road," having been constructed to reach some copper and other mines in the vicinity.

Yours, truly,
M. R. HULCE.

Extract from a Letter of C. L. Pascal, Esq.

MY DEAR SIR: It affords me much pleasure to comply with your request for the particulars in regard to the naming of Caldeno Falls.

In August, 1851, while on a visit to the Gap, it was my pleasure to make the acquaintance of Mr. Charles S. Ogden, of Philadelphia, a very pleasant and agreeable young man, and one quite as fond of rambling over the mountains as myself.

One day, after climbing to the top of the Jersey Mountain, we observed a charming little stream of water, and followed it down to the river below, rich in its falls, basins, troughs, and mossy grottos.

After dinner, while recounting the many beauties of this stream, and particularly its falls, to our host, your amiable brother William, he informed us that the beauty of stream and falls back on the Pennsylvania Mountain, far surpassed any we had seen. Not feeling inclined to doubt him, and anxious to see all the beauties of the Gap, we started eagerly in pursuit of it.

A Mr. McLeod accompanied us up the long steps, over the old mountain road, across the meadow, and up the steep cliff on the right, to the top of an extended flat rock, which inclined down to a continuous line of thicket, indicating the course of a stream leading towards the hotel, until we heard the thrilling music of falling water.

The scene was perfect. The grand old trees formed an arch above us, and as their branches were swayed by the breeze, bright patches of sunlight darted across the falling water.

Then it was suggested by one of the party that we should name the fall, and direct the attention of visitors to a spot so beautiful and so secluded.

Many names were proposed and rejected; finally

we concluded to form a new name out of syllables taken from our own, thus, "Cal" from Pas-cal; "den" from Og-den; and "o" from McLe-o-d. In this way, Cal-den-o Falls received its name.

Having refreshed ourselves, we climbed again to the top of the fall, then a little further on, we found a spot almost rivalling in its beauty the one we had just left.

Here we sat down and drank of the cold running stream, and were grateful to your brother for adding so much pleasure to our visit to the Water Gap.

And now, my good friend, I thank you for drawing my thoughts back over the years that have elapsed since Cal-den-o Falls was first known to me in all the wildness and grandeur it then possessed.

With great respect, I am, dear sir,

Your obedient servant,

Charles L. Pascal.

Philadelphia, April 4th, 1870.

www.ingramcontent.com/pod-product-compliance
Lightning Source LLC
LaVergne TN
LVHW010229110826
845151LV00004B/1239

* 9 7 8 1 4 2 5 5 2 5 6 4 4 *